#STAGNATION MUST FALL

ENDORSEMENTS

A must read for anyone serious about their career! I absolutely enjoyed immersing myself in this book and its 100 lessons. I was trying to think which ones were my favourites, but there are too many to mention. Siphiwe is hard-core, telling it like it is, saying all the things I wish someone had told me when I started out in my working life. I resonate with and believe in so much of what this book has to offer – I truly believe it should be a compulsory read for all!

Masenyane Molefe: Group Executive, Human Resources at PPS

Siphiwe has put together a wide-ranging travel guide for not merely surviving, but truly thriving throughout one's career in the organisational jungle. The guide is filled to the brim with practical wisdom. Not only does it draw skillfully on Siphiwe's own wide ranging experience, but it is also appropriately supplemented and enriched by an array of leading thinkers in the field. Without any doubt, this travel guide will make and keep one journey-ready and -fit, career-wise. It will also enhance the likelihood of having a successful and fulfilling career in the organisational jungle, which is filled with opportunities, dangers, threats and pitfalls.

Theo H Veldsman: Work Psychologist; Professor at the University of Johannesburg and University of Stellenbosch Business School

Do you ever feel stagnant in your career while your friends and colleagues are moving up the ladder? If you're struggling to find a career, get promoted, or get out of a job rut, #STAGNATIONMUSTFALL is the book you must take time to read. It will be the best investment that will help kick you into action. Siphiwe Moyo will guide you to take charge of your career and come out on top. He effectively dispenses, to both the young and old, some very straightforward yet thought provoking, smart, actionable career advice to help you navigate the world of work today and to gird yourself for success in the future.

Mr. *KC Makhubele (MBA): CEO of The South African Dental Association (SADA), a seasoned executive and business strategist who has been offering career advice for over 25 years*

Despite pockets of excellence, we live in a country in which mediocrity and stagnation have become the norm. At the macro level, economic growth has stagnated. At a micro level, people stagnate in their careers because of their own thinking and behaviour. In #StagnationMustFall, Siphiwe Moyo converted his personal experiences into an excellent work, consisting of 100 practical guidelines to turn stagnation around. The strength of the book lies in its practical wisdom expressed in succinct, yet profound, pieces of advice. You don't have to read this book front to back, although I have done so in two evenings only. You can use it as a quick reference guide in which to look for support for your specific demands.

The book challenges and navigates the reader through some of the often unspoken realities of corporate life, helping to dispel some of the myths that are holding you back from transforming yourself from stagnation to success.

Marius Meyer: Chairperson, SABPP;
Lecturer in HR Management, Stellenbosch University

Siphiwe has done it again by producing this masterpiece. If you like John Maxwell's work then you will love Siphiwe's. If you do not have at least twenty points talking directly to you, then my friend your career has crashed before take off. This is not an ordinary boring book. This is your success journal. Read it and read it again. Gift it to someone for it might not just save a dying career, but might make it flourish. Siphiwe is not just a writer, but speaks power and life to words and takes you to a zone where you discover the best of what you can still be career-wise. After all, it's in your hands, so future proof it!

Xolani Mawande: CEO, South African Board for People Practices

This book should be compulsory reading for absolutely everybody, whether you are a student, a worker, a manager or a politician. It is like having your own personal motivational speaker on hand 24/7. The format makes for easy reading and the personal experiences that Siphiwe shares gives it relevance in a time of increased economic despondency. When stagnation falls, excellence will rise. Not just personally, but in our communities and our beloved country.

Prof Pierre Joubert: Research Professor (Acting) Vaal University of Technology

Talent Management, Career Development and Performance Management is what I preach and breathe daily in my organisation. This book teaches you how you can progress and provides you with a different pair of glasses in terms of how you can visualise and structure your career path. It provides you with the necessary tools and steps to focus on the main things. This will be the best buy and a powerful tool that will help young professionals who just started their careers to progress beautifully. Thank you Mr Moyo for this insightful and powerful book.

Mpho Nkoane (BA Hons, MBA): Head, Human Resources,
MotoVantage (a division of FirstRand)

This book was like a flow of oxygen for me; a mental and social catalyst that is needed to shift, transform and uplift thinking patterns from our humdrum predictable selves and often self-imposed equilibrium to personal positive disruptor. The content is not subtle and nuanced; Siphiwe tells it like it is, through a fresh and unencumbered position of strength and growth mindset.The Siphiwe element in the content encourages gratitude, going the extra mile to achieve progress, and a call to action.

Lynette Naidoo: Talent Specialist

First published in 2019.

ISBN: 978-1-86922-806-4
eISBN: 978-1-86922-807-1

Published by KR Publishing
P O Box 3954
Randburg
2125

Republic of South Africa

Tel: (011) 706-6009
Fax: (011) 706-1127
E-mail: orders@knowres.co.za
Website: www.kr.co.za

Printed and bound: HartWood Digital Printing, 243 Alexandra Avenue, Halfway House, Midrand
Typesetting, layout and design: Cia Joubert, cia@knowres.co.za
Cover design: Cia Joubert, cia@knowres.co.za
Editing & proofreading: Jennifer Renton, jenniferrenton@live.co.za
Project management: Cia Joubert, cia@knowres.co.za
Index created with TExtract/www.Texyz.com

#STAGNATION MUST FALL

100 practical lessons that will activate your career progression

SIPHIWE MOYO

2019

ACKNOWLEDGEMENTS

To God, thank you so much for the gifts and talents that you have bestowed on me. Thank you for not giving up on me even when I had given up on myself. I recognise your hand on me and I'm truly humbled that you counted me worthy. Thank you.

A big thanks to my family for the encouragement, support and patience you showed me when this book was showing me flames. I appreciate you deeply. Thabzozo, you are incredible.

I would like to dedicate this book to Dr Ezekiel Mathole. All I ever wanted from the late 1990s was to lead like you, chair a meeting like you, speak like you, teach like you, be a lecturer like you, and more importantly, have the same character and integrity as you. You inspired me to have a huge vision. My aim now is to do for others what you did for me. I may not do it in the same office that you occupy, but I will do it using my gifts and talents, which is what you always encouraged me to do. I will forever endeavour to make you proud. Thank you.

CONTENTS

ABOUT THE AUTHOR

Siphiwe Moyo is a sought after, top-rated international keynote speaker, facilitator and author who is based in South Africa. He is an Adjunct Faculty member at GIBS, Henley and Wits business schools. Siphiwe is an Organisational Behaviour specialist who studies, teaches and speaks on employee ownership & accountability, leadership, personal & organisational change/transitions, personal development, employee motivation and team effectiveness.

He holds a Masters in Business Administration, an Executive Development Programme, a B Comm. (Honours) in People Development, a Bachelor's Degree (cum laude) in Human Resources and is currently completing his PhD in Organisational Behaviour. He is co-founder and Chief People Officer at Twice Blue (a human capital development firm), Past Chairman of the South African Board for People Practices (SABPP), Past Chapter President of the Professional Speakers Association of Southern Africa (PSASA) and is a member of the Global Speakers Federation.

Siphiwe is an author of three books, *Bulls & Bears: life lessons from the financial markets*, *#StagnationMustFall: 100 practical lessons that will activate your career progression* and *Via Midway: navigating personal & career transitions.*

INTRODUCTION

The day was 28 January 2014. It was 07:15 in the morning and I was a guest on a popular news and current affairs TV programme, *Morning Live*, on SABC 2. The interview was about Career Development/Career Progression, a subject matter I am extremely passionate about.

The interviewer, Leanne Manas, asked me: "So Siphiwe, is career development the responsibility of an employer or an employee?" My answer was that career development is definitely the employee's responsibility. I added that the employer may create frameworks and guidelines, but each and every one of us is responsible for our own career progression.

As I was driving back after that interview, I thought to myself: "There are too many people who genuinely believe that their career advancement is in their employer's hands and they wonder why they don't get the bursaries or promotions they believe they deserve." It was at this point that the idea of writing this book was born.

There is a well-known seTswana phrase in South Africa that says, "*Sesegolo ke bophelo*". The literal translation is: "The greatest is life." This obviously does not make sense, and to be honest that is not really what the phrase means. It means something like: "All that matters is that I'm still alive", or "Life is all that matters". I do not like this phrase at all; it is such a defeated statement. It is like saying, "I might be broke, miserable, sick, bored, disengaged and lonely, but hey, all that matters is that I'm still alive". No, that is not all that matters. Life is not about avoiding the negative, but about pursuing the positive. The absence of the negative does not necessarily mean the presence of the positive. The absence of misery does not necessarily mean the presence of happiness. The absence of disease does not necessarily mean the presence of health. The absence of sadness does not necessarily mean the presence of joy.

When you have been unemployed for a long time, all you want is a job; any job. You just want to get by. You want to survive. You want to earn a living and provide for yourself and your family. This is totally understandable.

Finding 'any' job means you have finally defeated unemployment (absence of the negative), but deep down you know that is not enough. People tell you that you should be grateful that the negative is absent and you are, but deep inside you sense that there should be more. You are right – there is more. What you're longing for is the presence of the positive.

You do not want to stick with a job that only helps you avoid the negative (unemployment and all the negatives that it brings such as starvation, alienation, anxiety and even sickness) – you want a job that makes you happy, and more importantly, a job where you can grow, advance, flourish and thrive. I am here to tell you that "survival" or "getting by" is not your destination. You are not going to stay there forever; you are just passing by. Thriving is your destination. This book will help you get out of stagnation, and advance, thrive and flourish in your career.

In this book, I will present 100 lessons that will help you progress in your career. Some of these lessons will deal with the attitudes required to progress, while some will be practical suggestions that you could use to advance your career and life immediately. As the author, John C. Maxwell, wrote: *"I can't think of anything worse than living a stagnant life, devoid of change and improvement."*[1]

The World of Work

Knowledge Resources recently published a great book about the new world of work[2], therefore the aim of this section is not to write extensively about the changing world of work, but to highlight the impact of it on our careers. There are a few things we know about the changing world of work:

- It is becoming more digital, global, diverse, automation-savvy, and social media proficient.[3]
- Organisations are becoming flatter, which means less traditional promotions. "Climbing the ladder" is largely being replaced by jungle gym (upwards, sideways, downwards, exit then come back) types of movements.
- Job security has become a myth. Employability, rather than employment, has become a source of security. Every employee should work hard to improve their employability while they are still employed. If you are not improving your skills and are not thinking about the future of your occupation, you are becoming less and less employable every day, and you might be one innovation away from becoming redundant.
- Long-term employment has also become a myth, or has it? This is something that is often said in conferences around the country, but it seems that this has remained constant over the last few years. The median number of years that wage and salary workers in the U.S. had been with their current employers was 4.2 years in January 2018, which was unchanged from January 2016.[4] In South Africa, this median tenure is 3.6 years.[5] What is becoming clear is that employees are staying with one employer but desire to do different jobs.
- New kinds of employment relationships are emerging as more and more people join the gig/freelance economy.
- Top line growth in many companies has become difficult to achieve, therefore there is a trend towards leaner organisations. In many companies now, when a manager leaves, they do not immediately replace them, but use the opportunity to evaluate if they still need that position. They might end up not replacing them at all, which is demoralising to the people who have been waiting for that role.

- The high unemployment rate in South Africa (27.5%, or over 36% if you consider the expanded definition of unemployment) means that people are holding on to jobs much longer, thereby reducing career mobility.
- There is not much loyalty on either side, and there is an increase in mutual separation agreements. I submit, however, that in the corporate world, we can no longer define 'loyalty' by the number of years people work for us; we need to ask whether people are fully present (engaged) while they are with us. Some of the most disloyal people never leave because they simply cannot find a job elsewhere. Better the people who resign and go than those who resign and stay. Most of my friends in corporate learning and development are telling me that they have started some kind of re-skilling and/or up-skilling initiatives in the organisations where they work. This is obviously in response to, and in anticipation of, the jobs that are/will be affected by technological disruptions. They also tell me that they are surprised by the slow uptake of employees to participate in these initiatives. Obviously they know that it is their responsibility to market these in their organisations, but I encourage you to reach out to your head of L&D or partner and proactively ask about these initiatives. If there is any re-skilling initiative at your work, make sure you volunteer to be part of it. Your future may depend on it.
- The augmented workforce. We are inundated by messages about Artificial Intelligence; robots that may or may not take our jobs. Although this should not necessarily scare us, it is clear that we must focus on increasing the value we provide our organisations.
- ***The overall responsibility for developing and enhancing careers is shifting more heavily to the employee. This is why this book is needed.***

I spend most of my time either chairing (emceeing) or speaking at conferences. There are always buzzwords/phrases that emerge in the conference circuit. The current phrase that is everywhere, particularly in government conferences but also in private sector conferences, is: *The*

Fourth Industrial Revolution. This is justified because we are all trying to understand its impact on the world of business, government and on our own careers. Probably the second most popular phrase in these conferences right now is the phrase "future-proof", which is obviously related to the first. When you future-proof something, you design it or change it so that it will continue to be useful or successful in the future if the situation changes. It is my responsibility to future-proof my career and it is your responsibility to do the same for yours. This book will help you to do exactly that.

"I can't think of anything worse than living a stagnant life, devoid of change and improvement."

(John C. Maxwell)[6]

Understand that things don’t just happen

You are the master of your own destiny

It was Thursday, 4 July 2002, at 04:30 in the morning. It was dark and it was cold. I was standing at a train station in Orange Farm called Stretford, waiting for the second Metrorail train of the day travelling from Vereeniging to Johannesburg, train number 9003, which was due to arrive at 04:44am. I was doing an internship in Braamfontein at a company called Mining Qualifications Authority.

While waiting for the train, a friend of mine who was standing next to me said: "Siphiwe, this thing of waking up so early in the cold and rushing for a train, must stop. We must work hard, buy ourselves homes and cars and get out of this informal settlement." I was very inspired by this and was in complete agreement.

Many years later, I went back to Orange Farm and was very sad to discover that my friend was still travelling on the same Metrorail train from Vereeniging to Johannesburg.

When I asked him what had happened to our dream of leaving Orange Farm for a better life, he said something that was the inspiration for me to write this book: "Siphiwe, the system has blocked me from achieving that dream. The system has marginalised and ostracised us. The government that we have elected has neglected us. They eat alone and have forgotten about the people who voted for them. No one wants to give us tenders or even bursaries my friend. Spijo (this is what he called me), you're lucky that you managed to get out of this place."

I was shattered when I heard my friend utter those words. I know that he was to a certain extent raising legitimate issues, and I am not at all trying to discredit his sentiments, but I believe that his thinking was flawed. Many other people who grew up in the same environment and under similar circumstances as us still managed to rise above the obstacles and achieve greater things.

My friend missed an opportunity in this regard; he needed to understand one of the most significant life lessons, i.e. **things do not just happen**. When I convinced him that this mind-set was limiting his and many other people's progress, he gladly agreed to let me share his story. I set myself a goal to not only help my friend, but to also help all those who possess this limiting mentality, by writing this book and sharing his story in this chapter. If there is only one thing you get out of this book, I hope it is this: If you are going to achieve progress in your career, you have to understand this critical fact – nothing just happens. We make things happen, intentionally so. **Lives are not changed by intentions but by actions.**

Many people misunderstand (intentionally or otherwise) what those of us who advocate for the "take responsibility for your career" narrative are actually saying. We are misconstrued as being ahistorical and acontextual, and ignoring the reality around us. This is not what we are saying, or at least it is not what I'm saying.

- Of course it matters where you were born, because some regions of the world have more access to resources than others.
- The hand you were dealt by life matters; some people are dealt better cards than others.
- Of course the political environment in a country matters; political risk is a real thing. We should care about how our government spends our money, because without fiscal discipline you have sovereign risk, country risk and consequently we risk our independence as a country.

On an organisational level, we should admit that there are other things that happen in an organisation that are way beyond our pay grade – things we cannot control.

So I am not ahistorical or acontextual; I know these things matter. I need to make a clear differentiation, however... the fact that I was not responsible for CAUSING something, does not mean that I cannot take responsibility for changing it. Even if you did not cause a recession, you still need to run a business in tough trading conditions. It is not my fault that I grew up in a poor informal settlement called Orange Farm, but I needed to take responsibility and say, "I won't end up here". It is very empowering to know that I can do something about my circumstances.

Ultimately, you get to decide if you want to be the master of your own destiny.

Do not despise small beginnings

Starting small should push you to want and pursue your big dreams

When I started studying for my first degree in 1999, I realised very quickly that even though the National Student Financial Aid Scheme (NSFAS) was paying for my tuition, I still needed money to travel to campus and for other basic needs such as food. I went to look for a job and fortunately found part-time work at a Mr Price clothing store in Southgate Mall, Johannesburg. I do not know what their wages are currently, but a casual employee's salary was very low then; I only earned about R60 per day, yet I still managed to maintain an enthusiastic attitude in the three-year period I worked there.

There is someone I have been helping for a long time with groceries and money; let us call him Jimmy. I recently decided to help Jimmy find a job, which I did. Before completing the first month, Jimmy told me that he wanted to quit because, "I can't work for R150 per day". As I mentioned, when I started working in 1999, I earned R60 a day. Assuming a 6% annual interest rate, this would be R152.45 today. This means that I worked for three years for almost the same amount of money that Jimmy felt he could not work for. I know I cannot force him to work, but if he quits, he must never even think of calling me again for help.

I know you know people who have shared similar sentiments as Jimmy. I hope you do not partake in this nor possess this mind-set, because if you do, you still have a very long way to go in your life and career, my friend. We live in a society where people are only interested in the great end result and not the small beginnings; people want to be like you, yet could care less about what it took to get you where you are.

It appears that somehow people feel they are too big, too smart, too special and/or too powerful to start small. This 'go big or go home' attitude has become so predominant that it is ruining us. We are all too quick to celebrate only significant achievements, not noticing the smaller ones as they are not wrapped in fancy packages.

Let me use this opportunity to highlight the paradox of hedonism, or simply put, the paradox of happiness or pleasure, from positive psychology. This phenomenon states that we believe that the more we get what we want, in this instance pleasure, such as from a promotion, the happier we will be. In fact, pursuing what we want (pleasure/promotion) is futile, because we will never get enough as long as that pleasure or happiness is external.

Think of it this way; when you are unemployed, your major concern is getting a job, yet when you eventually get a junior position that pays you about R5,000, you want R8,000, and eventually that is also insufficient so you pursue R10,000, and so it goes on. What a human condition we possess!

The key point I am trying to make here is simple. In order to get to Point C, it makes logical sense to start at Point A and follow the steps. In this way, if you want to earn R15,000, then at some point, R5,000 to R8,000 should not be a problem. It is better and smarter to endure the lower amount for a certain period as it channels you to the desired amount, rather than quitting because you are not getting what you want, when you want it.

I believe all we really need to do is to grow up and stop acting like kids trapped in adults' bodies. This whole 'instant gratification' phase really needs to be done with by the time we reach adolescence. Instant gratification, i.e. starting big and always getting what we feel we deserve, is just not how life works. Well at least for the most part!

We all start somewhere, so do not despise your small beginnings; they may appear small and insignificant, but the end result will be greater. Indeed, you have the potential to shock those who think you are limited to where you are. Above all, you have the potential to shock yourself by ending up where you never thought you could be. It is possible, and your small beginnings should not be a disadvantage. If anything, starting small should push you to want and pursue your big dreams relentlessly.

Be dissatisfied with your current level

> *"If what you did yesterday still looks big to you; you haven't done much today"*
>
> (Elbert Hubbard)[6]

Some of my previous points may give the impression that I believe you should be satisfied with where you are. On the contrary – we ought to be dissatisfied with the level we are currently at in order to get ahead. According to Rick Warren, "The greatest enemy of tomorrow's success is today's success".[8]

You have to be dissatisfied with your current role if you want to move forward. I used to take this for granted until I learnt that some people do not actually want to move; they do not aspire for more. They are simply okay doing what they are doing, which is fine, but if you want more, if you really want to move to the next level, you have to have a healthy level of discontentment because you cannot move if you are satisfied.

To qualify my statement let me just say this... being dissatisfied is not the same as complaining, moaning, dreading your job and doing whatever it takes to show your bosses and colleagues how unhappy and miserable you are. For some reason, we tend to think this gives a loud and clear message to our managers, but if anything, it actually makes very little room for advancement and improvement in our careers. Therefore, discontentment in this instance does not equate to any of these negative characteristics. Healthy levels of dissatisfaction involve a combination of negative and positive aspects of your current level that push you to aspire for more, with the negative elements dominated by the positive elements.

> *"Something in human nature tempts us to stay where we are comfortable. We try to find a plateau, a resting place, where we have comfortable stress and adequate finances. Where we have comfortable associations with people, without the intimidation of meeting new people and entering strange situations."*
>
> (John Maxwell)[9]

Mastering the art of wanting more while still performing in your current role

Ambition and gratitude are not mutually exclusive

The biggest career mistake we make? Neglecting our 'current' while pursuing our 'next'. It is possible to aspire for more and still look after what you have now. If, for example, you are currently playing for Burnley F.C. in the English Premier League, but believe you should be playing for Man City, that is okay. But if you slack off at Burnley because you think they do not deserve you, not only will you not fulfil your dream of playing for Man City, but Burnley will get rid of you. You are not doing your current employer a favour – they are paying you a salary, so give it your best even if you know there is more to you than what you are currently doing.

The best job is when you operate in the sweet spot between boredom (comfort zone) and constant trepidation (panic zone). This stretch zone is the optimum zone that we all should want to be in. What I have learnt, however, is that if you do not perform in your current job because you feel stagnant, you are going to have a bigger problem... unemployment.

What career zone are you currently in?[10]

Stagnation Zone	Restless, antsy, trapped, anxious, or bored. May start manifesting as physical symptoms and health problems.
Comfort Zone	Feeling good about the status quo; daily life does not demand much deep thinking about the direction of your career. Work is "fine".
Stretch Zone	Challenged, excited and motivated to get out of bed every day. Actively learning: work may be unpredictable, but you feel engaged.
Panic Zone	Anxiety is starting to dominate your thoughts; you are not able to think long term about the future because you are dealing with things that are "on fire" in your day-to-day life. Or, if contemplating next steps, you feel so paralysed by fear that you end up doing nothing.

I know you want more, and that is okay. Ambition and gratitude are not mutually exclusive. You can be grateful that you have a job and still know deep down that you want more in life – there is nothing wrong with this. The main thing is that you should still perform in your current job, otherwise you will not have the job/business you want and you will lose the one you have.

Lose the job description mentality

Sometimes it is the so-called "menial" tasks that will activate your career progression

I have told you the story about my friend and I waiting for a train. Allow me now to give you a bit more detail about my engagements that year. As mentioned earlier, I was an intern at the Mining Qualifications Authority (MQA), which is a Sector Education & Training Authority (SETA) for the mining industry in South Africa. As far as I can remember, this was the first time the MQA had hired interns. Being an intern obviously means that you are the most low-ranking person in the organisation, which implies that different people ask you to do all kinds of things.

One of the main tasks of the MQA was to organise skills development conferences in the mining sector. As interns (there were a few of us), we would be asked to assist with carrying boxes to and from the conference centres. We were, however, given a choice in this, as it was not in our job description. Some of my fellow interns refused to do these tasks, as they felt they were demeaning when they had Human Resources degrees. I also had a Human Resources degree, but I chose to do it regardless.

What my fellow interns did not realise was that when you helped to take boxes to a conference and later returned them to the office, you got to attend the conferences in between. As an intern, I was therefore attending conferences and was exposed to discussions that were way ahead of my position.

In 2012, I was elected as Chairman of the South African Board for People Practices (SABPP), the professional body for Human Resource professionals in South Africa. Can you imagine what a shock this was to my friends? I can imagine how jaw dropping such unforeseen news must have been. As far as I know, I was the youngest ever Chairman of the SABPP. What an honour! I believe the discussions I was exposed to as an intern contributed to this. Sometimes it is the so-called "menial" tasks that will activate your career progression. You may never know what will contribute to your upward mobility, so forget the job description – it will limit your progress.

The differences between a positive and a negative attitude[11]

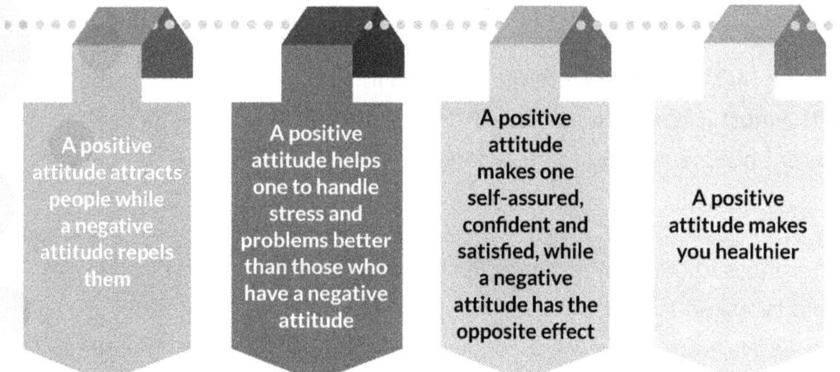

Get rid of fear

In order to move to the next level, fear must fall

The reason many people do not progress is that they are afraid. As Dostoevsky put it, "Taking a new step, uttering a new word, is what most people fear most".[12]

Do not be afraid of failure. In order to move to the next level, fear must fall.

> *"The person interested in success has to learn to view failure as a healthy, inevitable part of the process of getting to the top."*
>
> (Dr Joyce Brothers)[13]

In his book, *The Psychology of Achievement*, Brian Tracy[14] wrote about four millionaires who had made their fortunes by the time they were 35. They were involved in an average of 17 businesses each before they found the one that took them to the top. They kept on trying and changing until they found something that worked for them.

In her book, *Pivot*, the co-creator of Google's Career Guru programme, Jenny Blake, identified four career operating modes that all of us could adopt.[15]

I would certainly love to see you operating in the 'innovative' mode where you have a clear career strategy. Imagine being in a job which you can describe in this way: "...being completely involved in an activity for its own sake. The ego falls away. Time flies. Every action, movement, and thought follows inevitably from the previous one, like playing jazz. Your whole being is involved, and you're using your skills to the utmost."[16] That, ladies and gentlemen, is what positive psychologist, Mihaly Csikszentmihalyi, calls a "state of flow", and it is highly possible.

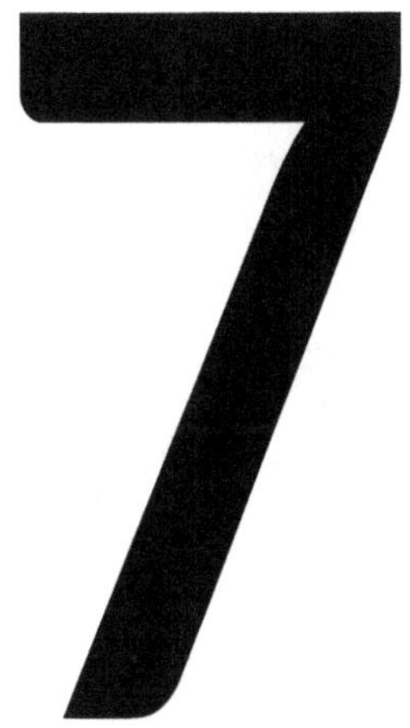

Understand that someone is always watching how you perform the small tasks

"We have watched how you did all the small tasks and therefore believe you can do the big tasks."

I am a sought-after professional speaker now, but I can assure you that it has not always been that way. In 2011, while I was still working for one of the big banks, I decided that I wanted a career in professional speaking and to make it my way of earning a living. Before I resigned, I joined the Professional Speakers Association of Southern Africa (PSASA) as an associate member, as I did not qualify at that time to be a professional member.

One of the things I did after joining the PSASA was volunteer to do the tasks that most members did not want to do: handle the registration desk, set up before the meetings, and pack things away after our meetings. Ask anybody at the PSASA and they will tell you that these are the most dreaded tasks in the organisation. I continued doing these tasks for a while, faithfully so and to the best of my abilities. Excellence is a practice after all. It was in 2014 when I was surprised to be elected as the Gauteng Chapter President of this amazing association. The person who nominated me said the following: "We have watched how you did all the small tasks and therefore believe you can do the big tasks." This statement humbled me because it is a lesson I was taught as a young man – to be faithful in the little things.

The lesson in all this is... whether you see them or not, whether you are aware of it or not, please know that someone is watching as you do those small tasks. Do yourself a favour and do them to the best of your ability. You may be working in obscurity, nobody may know your name and sometimes people might not even greet you, but be faithful in those tasks because someone is always watching.

Nobody owes you a promotion

Promotions are about current efforts and achievements

Some people believe that their company owes them a promotion. Now, as I said, I am a Human Resources graduate and I know a bit about our country's labour laws, so I can confirm that nobody in your organisation owes you a promotion. If you are going to get one, it will be because you work hard and nothing else. YOU must raise YOUR hand.

It does not matter how long you have been with your company, nor does it matter how much you have done for them. The clients you signed on years ago, or whatever legitimate and valid reasons you may give to justify your entitlement, do not matter. Promotions are about current efforts and achievements, and nothing besides hard work and going the extra mile are good enough to get you promoted.

I will never forget the one-on-one discussion about talent I had in November 2016 with the then CEO of Sun International, Graeme Stephens, in his Sandton office. I was very curious how a busy executive of a large business that has multiple properties identified talent. How did he know if there was some bright spark in Sun City in the North West province, in Boardwalk in Port Elizabeth or the Wild Coast Sun in Port Edward? He told me in no uncertain terms that he did not have time to identify talent – he had a business to run. If someone is talent, he said, they must not wait to be discovered, but must raise their own hand. Talent should strike you in the face, he added; it must be so obvious that you have no choice but to recognise it.

My friend, no one is coming to discover you. It is totally up to you to raise your hand and make yourself noticeable by performing.

Pay the price for progress

Do not let people fool you into this quick fix mind-set

A story is often told about the famous artist, Pablo Picasso. "One day a woman spotted him in the market and pulled out a piece of paper, 'Mr. Picasso,' she said excitedly, 'I'm a big fan. Please, could you do a little drawing for me?' Picasso happily complied and quickly etched out a piece of art for her on the paper provided. He smiled as he handed it back to her and said, 'That will be a million dollars.' 'But Mr. Picasso,' the flustered woman replied, 'It only took you 30 seconds to do this little masterpiece.' 'My good woman,' Picasso laughed, 'It took me 30 years to know how to do that masterpiece in 30 seconds.'

There is absolutely no such thing as instant success. There is no ready mix or instant porridge when it comes to success; do not let people fool you into this quick fix mind-set.

The people that we celebrate now have been paying the price for a long time. We all have to pay the price to excel and succeed. Have a healthy work ethic, put in the hours, and commit yourself to your own learning, development and growth. Sacrifice the unnecessary outings, TV shows, social media and other time-wasting activities that steal your valuable time. That is how you pay the price for your progress.

> *"You can't have a million-dollar dream and a minimum wage work ethic."*
>
> (Stephen C. Hogan)[17]

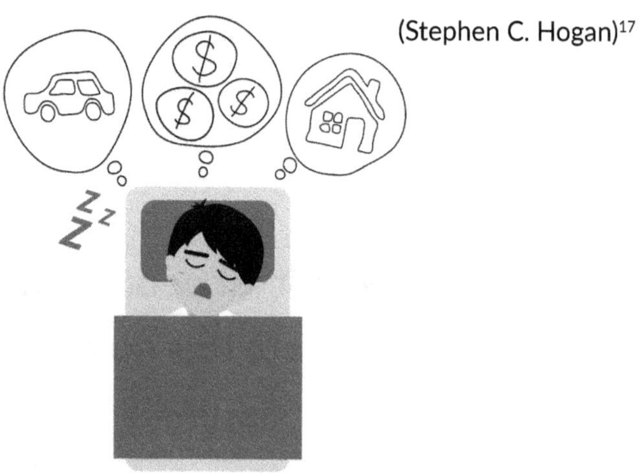

10

The principle of forward-looking preparation

If you want to change your position and state of affairs, start in your mind

I love listening to the radio during the holiday season because the main DJs/hosts are not there. In this period, you are bound to discover some brilliant talent who usually work in some strange hours of the morning. This is how I always see and think of it: whatever opportunity you want, the main person is bound to go on holiday, get sick or something of the sort. The question is not whether that day will come, but whether you will be ready when that opportunity comes?

John Maxwell put it this way: "When opportunity comes, it's too late to prepare."[18] Read up on most artists and how they were discovered, and you will find that despite auditions that were prepared for with much work and effort, there are also beautiful stories of 'random selections', which we know are not so random. If you want to be a manager at some point, you will need to exhibit your management qualities and style before the role will be given to you.

I strongly advise everyone, intern or manager, to read *Leading without a Title* by Robin Sharma. You can thank me later! The book teaches one of the most significant lessons in life, i.e. you do not need to be what you want to be to start acting like it. In fact, you can act like it before you become it, so that by the time you officially become it, the processes and adjustments are seamless. You see, leadership is a state of mind, not a state of position.

Set your mind right and position it into leadership first before you need to act and live it out, and the challenges will be easily surmountable. This applies to all sorts of things we want in life. It may sound overrated, but how you think and what you set and engage your brilliant mind upon determines who you become and what you possess. You may have heard the saying: you are what you think. Even now, wherever you are, if you feel lost and unsure how to reach your destination, simply trace your thoughts and you will get your answer.

Likewise, if you want to change your position and state of affairs, start in your mind. It really is that simple, and it is never too late my friend. There is absolutely nothing the mind can fail at, despite what we limit it to and the boundaries we set through our thoughts. Do not be the reason for your stagnancy; deliberately channel yourself and set yourself up for success in a top-down fashion – from your mind to your actions and eventually your habits.

The habit loop[19]

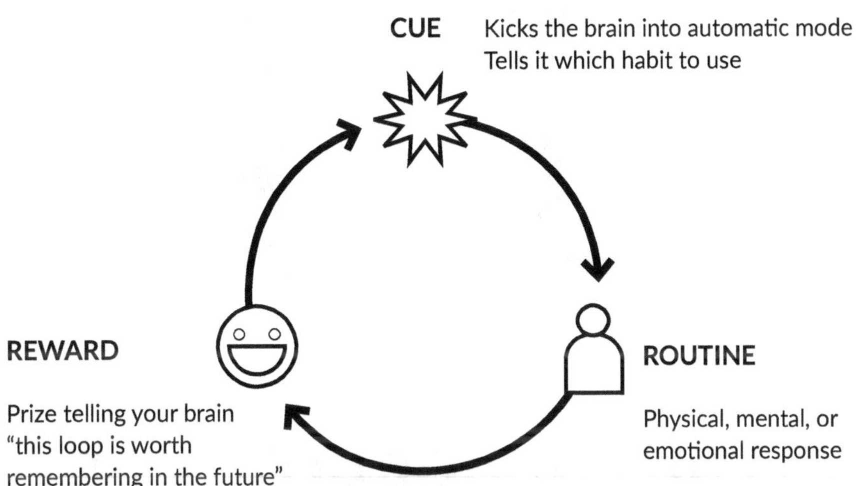

You cannot progress in your life and career without sacrifice

Dreams do come true, if only we wish hard enough

It is normal for entrepreneurs to downgrade or even sell their cars to start a business. The logic is simple really; if you cannot even downgrade your car to follow your dream, then you simply do not want it enough. Many people have had to sacrifice far more than a car downgrade.

Strive Masiyiwa, a telecoms billionaire, tells a fascinating story about how he financed his business. He started his journey in 1986 with just US$75, going around suburbs fixing broken lights and gates. After running the business for a while, he needed additional funding so he went to a Barclays bank branch seeking a loan. He drove his car, parked it outside the bank and went in to pitch the banker. "After listening to my pitch, she asked, 'Is that your car?'" He replied in the affirmative and she responded, "Go sell it and I will match whatever it is you sell it for. That is my way of knowing whether you are serious or not." "So, I took my car away… I sold it and I came back the following day. I had the money in cash, I put it on her table and I said: 'Where is yours?' And I haven't looked back ever since."

"Dreams do come true, if only we wish hard enough. You can have anything in life if you will sacrifice everything else for it."

(J.M. Barrie)[20]

Sacrifice is a prerequisite to success. "If you don't sacrifice for what you want then what you want will be the sacrifice."[21] Be willing to lose something for a greater gain; sacrifice!

12

People who are too nice to you will limit your career progress

Managers invest in potential; accept constructive criticism

When I was working at the MQA, the Chief Executive Officer was the late Dr Menzi Mthwecu. When my boss started becoming comfortable with my work, he said I could submit it directly to him. Every time I sent something to him, he would print it and then use his red pen to make all kinds of corrections, in what seemed to be an extremely rude manner. In addition, he would often tell me that I had wasted his time by submitting such "nonsense" to him.

For a while I thought he really hated me until one day, he called me into his office and said to me, "You know why I'm very hard on you?" I was standing there thinking, "Oh, he actually knows he's hard on me", when he said, "I'm hard on you because I think you have potential. If I didn't think so, I would not waste my time on you. I would just ask Chernice (my direct manager) to stop allowing you to deal directly with me. I think you're going to be a leader in the skills development arena".

The bottom line is this: a manager who is too understanding when you produce sloppy work actually thinks it is not worth their time to correct you. Managers invest in potential, so if you feel yours is pushing you towards your limit and overworking you, instead of complaining and grumbling, thank them and allow yourself to fully utilise, explore and exploit your potential. Aim to excel and accept constructive criticism with humility and a smile on your face, knowing that you are worth their time.

13

Exposure propels progress

Hang around with the optimists and the hard workers

Some people are no longer progressing in their careers because they spend too much time with people who admire them. They strongly possess a "Mama I made it" mentality, yet they can go much further. Thoughts and statements such as "I'm the man", "I'm the only one with a degree in my family" and "I've been the first in getting the best things in life within my network" are seriously hampering their progress.

I remember in 2009 when I began showing symptoms of this type of mind-set. You see, I had left Orange Farm and was staying in a middle-class suburb; every time I went home on the weekends, people would tell me how much I inspired them. This happened for a long time, until one evening, I was going to a meeting in a place called Atholl in Sandton. It was one of those meetings held in someone's house. I still remember my arrival as though it was yesterday; they opened a gate for me and the first thing I saw in the yard was a tennis court. I could not believe I was seeing a tennis court in someone's backyard. I remember asking my fellow traveller, "Dude, is this like the community tennis court?" My friend just said, "Siphiwe, please don't embarrass me!"

When we finally got to the house, we were escorted to one of the rooms; I'm not sure what it is called. Please accommodate me here – remember that black people in South Africa still refer to a lounge as a dining room. So, taking this into consideration, there I was, in a house with four different rooms that all had couches. I was not sure whether I should sit, kneel, and lift my hands in worship or what? That was when I had an awakening. It hit me that day that I was not as successful as I thought I was; that I was not as successful as my friends in Orange Farm thought I was. I had not made it yet!

At that point, my dream changed. I had seen better; I had seen something to aspire to. I know that it was a very material thing, but I learnt a valuable lesson that day; exposure does change your dreams and ambitions – it changes your definition of success. If you are no longer hungry for more, check what and who you are exposed to. It is possible that you are spending too much time with people who adore you too much.

There is such a strong power we seem to dismiss in the workplace – the power of associations. You see, if you hang around the complainers, gossipers and lazy bones, you may not be one of them yet, but sooner or later you most likely will be. Likewise, if you want to be evaluated in a positive light, hang around with the optimists, the hard workers and the bosses' favourites; it will put you in a very good place.

14

Do not rely on networking and relationships; you still need to perform

Relate well with people, network, make contacts and maintain positive relationships

"It's not what you know, it's who you know." Fair enough, but I personally think this statement is ridiculously overused. What you know is actually very important to progress in your career. Many South Africans who get jobs in the corporate sector do not know anyone in those organisations. In fact, most of the jobs I have ever had in my career are jobs I got because I applied through the normal channels and my application met the necessary requirements.

I say 'most' because obviously in internal company positions, people get to know you and what you can do, which is a different matter altogether. I do agree that relationships and networks are important to get ahead, but I think we tend to exaggerate the role they play in career progression. I mean, even if someone puts in your CV, it still needs to look good and you still need to impress in the interview. Most significantly though, once you are offered that job, you must deliver. So do not be deceived, because what you know is still very important to get ahead.

In summary, relate well with people, network, make contacts and maintain positive relationships, but above all, know your job and do it well. It is critical that you never rely for your success on people alone. Concentration risk is a banking term that describes the level of risk in a bank's portfolio that arises from concentration on a single client type, sector or country. I believe there is also career concentration risk; if your entire career is dependent on one person remaining a CEO or manager, you have high concentration risk and you might be in trouble. If your business is dependent on one person remaining the premier/minister in government, you might be in trouble. You have to diversify.

15

Your boss does have favourites; they are called good performers

Bosses favour exceptional performers

As someone who worked in Human Resource Development for a long time, a complaint I often dealt with was this: "Our boss only listens to her blue-eyed boy and no one else." In fact, if I am honest, I have uttered this kind of statement myself. At certain points, it seemed to me and many others that a manager just decided to favour one person over another, until I observed something... I had an 'aha' moment when I realised that almost all the bosses' favourites were exceptional performers.

There may be one crazy manager who has favourites based on other criteria, but in the main, it is because that employee works extremely hard and continually makes their manager look good. Try it and thank me later.

16

Understand that your boss will take credit for your work; that is just how it goes

Stop complaining about the petty inevitable things

Many people do not get this; they often come to us and complain about their managers taking credit for their work. They whisper things like, "You know I actually created that strategy and all he did was present it, and now he's acting like it was all his idea." Well, in case you did not know, let me brief you about your manager's role – the job of a manager is to get results through other people. You should therefore be very happy and pleased if your manager presents your work as it is, because it shows the confidence they have in you.

Can we please stop complaining about the petty inevitable things? Managers do not fundamentally exist to create and come up with the work; they exist to facilitate it. The sooner you accept this, the happier you will be on your career journey.

"Management is an art of getting things done through people."[22]

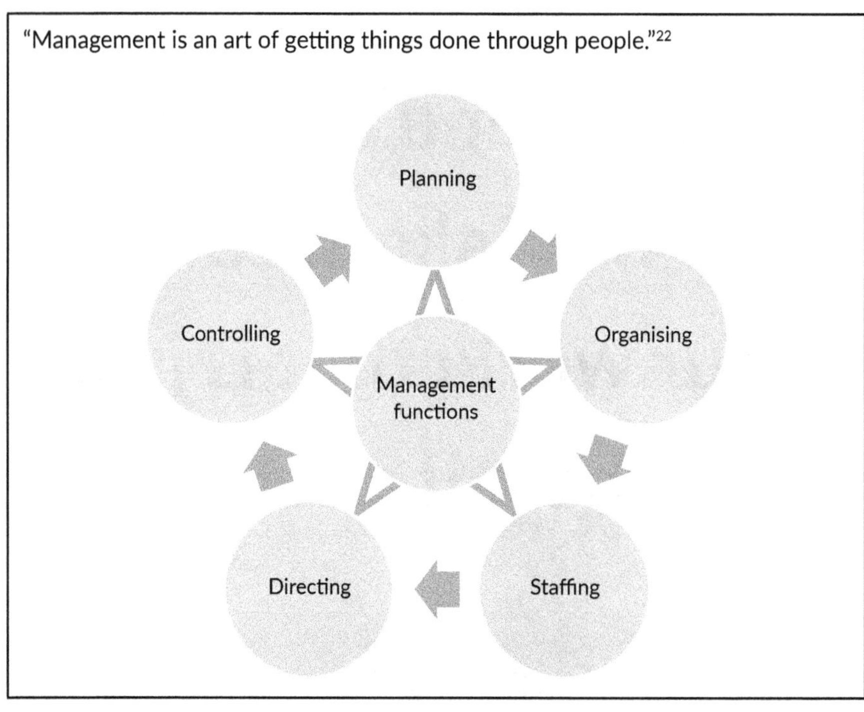

17

Never try to outshine your boss – you will not win

"Always say less than necessary"

(Robert Greene)[22]

Many years ago, I read a book entitled, *The 48 Laws of Power*, by Robert Greene. The very first lesson I read was to never outshine your master. Contrary to popular belief, all of us have a responsibility to ensure that those above us feel comfortably superior. You should therefore do everything possible to make sure that your boss does not see you as someone trying to be smarter than him – trust me, it is a bad idea and you will live to regret it.

In your defence, I understand how it may be difficult to carry out such duties; as some managers make it hard, you may easily opt to outshine them. Your colleagues may cheer you for this, but please bear in mind that in the end, whether you are outshining your boss out of spite, because they deserve it, or any other reason, it will essentially do more harm to you than good. Ask anyone who has tried this or made any other attempts to paint a negative picture of their boss and they will tell you, whether they were right or wrong, it just never ends well my friend. Therefore, never set out on this doomed mission as it will only explode in your face, not your boss'.

18

Contrary to popular belief, your boss and your senior leadership actually want yes-men/-women on their team

You are not paid to oppose

I think many people engage in a lot of self-deception by saying things like, “My boss does not want a yes-man/-woman, he wants us to challenge him.” Really? Let me be straight on this one: every boss wants team members who say “yes” more than they say “no”. Nobody wants a ‘Mmusi Maimane’ in their team. For those who do not know, Mmusi Maimane is the leader of the official opposition party in South Africa, the Democratic Alliance (DA).

People need to understand that a person like Mmusi is actually paid to oppose. You, on the other hand, are not. I am not suggesting you say “yes” all the time, but I guarantee you, saying “yes” more than you say “no” will work out to your advantage.

19

You must earn the right to differ with your boss; if you are not an exceptional performer, keep quiet and do as you are told

Prove yourself worthy

If you are not fully functioning in your role, you must keep quiet and do what you are told to do. Sometimes you find people who are not performers thinking they can just challenge their bosses. Do your job first, and then you will earn your boss' ear regarding a different way of doing things. You are not entitled to an opinion if you have not earned it. Prove yourself worthy of the position and you will be worth hearing and your points regarded as noteworthy. Until then, your lack of performance and reputation as a low or average performer will always serve as a hindrance.

20

If you and your boss have a different opinion on how something should be done, do it the way your boss wants it; you are not the boss!

You do not have to agree with it, you just have to do it

Once upon a time, I had a colleague who used to have unnecessary arguments with our boss. She would insist that the template in which the boss wanted her reports to be done did not make sense. She argued that there was a better way of submitting those reports and she was quite vocal about it.

Here is a noteworthy fact: in the workplace, things such as report templates are merely a matter of preference, and as an employee, you have no authority to determine how they should be done. Your preference is not more important than that of the boss, so kindly spare us the drama and submit them the way your boss prefers and wants them. If you keep arguing with your boss about such things, you create unnecessary tension between the two of you and that will hamper your progression.

I am not saying you should never disagree with your boss, but some things are just a matter of preference, so you need to accept that. Unfortunately, it is one of those 'because I said so' kinds of situations. If you and your boss have a different opinion on how something should be done, simply do it the way your boss wants it and withdraw your case. It is that simple really – you do not have to agree with it, you just have to do it.

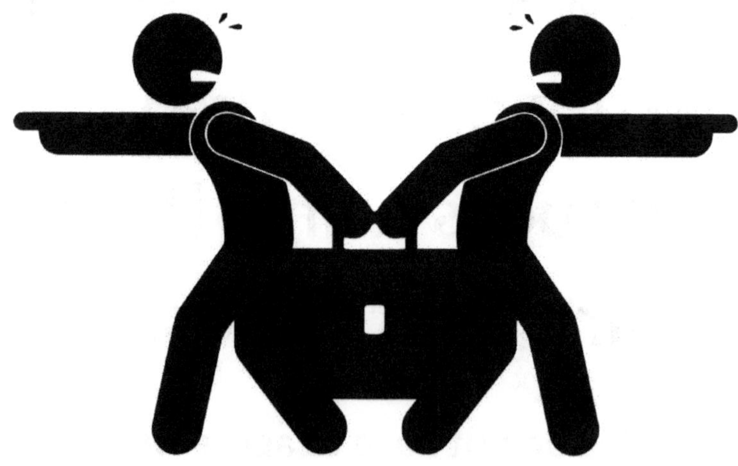

21

Do not be a high maintenance employee; you are there to make life easier for your bosses, not more difficult

If you are high maintenance, you are disposable

No manager wants to have a high maintenance employee. They are way too needy and behave like a child trapped in an adult's body. They moan, they groan, and they want special attention and treatment all the time. Some people are always taking leave for this and that and ask for all kinds of favours; they have all sorts of things they expect their managers and colleagues to understand. They have enough problems and work cannot add onto their stress.

I will let you in on a little secret. For those of you who have never worked in HR, please allow me to tell you that if you are abusing sick leave, your manager knows. If you get sick every time you have to make a decision, how do you expect to be given a position where you will have to make decisions every hour? You will never be considered for any form of promotion if you keep going like that. You will do all that you do and have always done for decades; the same chair, same desk, same tasks and all. Your working days will seem like a movie on replay; no new challenges, no new roles.

Let me add this, if you are high maintenance, you are easily disposable. Why should your employer hold onto you when you give them no reason to? If anything, you keep proving how expensive you are and what a loss and waste of the company's resources and benefits you are. You see the basic 'tit for tat' rule always applies, even at work.

Do not be high maintenance my friend; it will hamper your chances of progression. You are actually employed to make your manager's life easier, not more difficult. Stop with the excuses now and rebuild your reputation.

22

The 'open door policy' does not mean the door is open all the time

Only go to your manager's desk when necessary

Many organisations have open plan offices these days, which is becoming a problem as some employees fail to understand this simple phenomenon: the fact that your manager is at her desk does not mean she is available for you. Let me break the news; having an employee who constantly comes to your desk unannounced is disturbing and awfully irritating. I know for a fact that most things are never that urgent, so if the building is not burning and the client is not threatening to switch agencies, then it can wait.

If you do not want to be a nuisance to your boss, here is my advice: learn to write a list of all you need clarity on and get all your stories and points straight, then you can schedule a 15 to 30-minute session or meeting with your manager as an appropriate platform to have a discussion with her. The point here is to only go to your manager's desk when necessary.

23

Always make your boss look good – always

Let your boss shine in your spotlight

If you want to get ahead in your career, it means someday you want to be someone's boss as well. The principle here is simple, apply the Golden Rule: do unto others as you would like them to do unto you. Treat your boss as you would want your subordinates to treat you; in how you address and represent them, and in your attitude, work ethic and basic human courtesy.

Whether they deserve it or not, do not dehumanise your boss into a monster, as that will hinder you from treating them with respect and having a good working relationship with them, which will in turn block your progress. Imagine the effort it takes to be mean and spiteful to your boss. Is it not easier to make them look good instead? Speak highly of them, let them take the credit, *let them shine in your spotlight*; that is why he or she is the boss and that is why you will be soon.

24

Take initiative

Think outside of the box

"One of the fastest ways to put your career onto the fast track, to become more valuable, is to develop and maintain the power of initiative."

(Brian Tracy)[24]

Nothing says 'You got this!' like taking the right initiative in your work. I say right initiative because unfortunately there is such a thing as wrong initiative, which can do far more harm than good to your career. If your manager is not around to make a certain call and you make a wrong or uninformed decision, or you make what appears to be a right and smart decision to you, only to have it bite you later on because it was not so right after all, that is the wrong initiative.

Unfortunately, most of us are so concerned with proving our ability to take initiative that sometimes we cut corners and apply certain measures that do not comply with our industry's or company's systems, processes and even policies. Taking the right initiative requires a thorough assessment of the case and implementation of proven methods. You do not have to invent to prove you can take initiative; you can do what your manager would do and maybe do it better, smarter and more efficiently.

However, sometimes one does need to take risks, and the truth is that very few things offer you the ability to take risks in the work environment as the opportunity to take initiative does. In such a case, ensure that whatever you are about to do will not come back to hurt you; employ all the necessary measures and ensure that your innovative strategy has been tested to effectively solve the issue at hand.

I think I have made the point I wanted to make in this chapter, but I will rephrase it nonetheless. Taking initiative is necessary for your career growth; it shows you can manage your work and that you can think out of the box. It shows you can handle responsibility and successfully complete your tasks. Taking initiative will definitely build your reputation as innovative, creative and hardworking, which will absolutely score you some great points and enhance your chances of career advancement and promotion.

However, taking initiative also comes with the responsibility to adhere to systems and processes. Moreover, it requires confidence in your implementation, and depending on the risks involved, the guaranteed success of your ideas or methods in order for them to work, instead of against, you.

Please remember that sometimes when you are required to take initiative it may be on smaller tasks and therefore thinking on your feet is required. At such times, elements such as innovation and creativity may not necessarily come into play, which is okay because sometimes it really is just about making a seemingly obvious decision or presenting a simple idea. The point is to ensure that whatever you suggest or implement is relevant and effective for your project, and that it will be fruitful and produce the desired outcome.

25

Sometimes you will feel goose bumps when you work and sometimes you will not. It is called work for a reason. Just do it!

Only immature people wait for inspiration before they work

Producing sloppy work that lacks creativity and passion as a result of your lack of inspiration and interest is plain immaturity. Remember how in school you had to pass a module whether you liked and enjoyed it or not? Remember how whether the lecturer was boring or exciting made no difference to the fact that you still needed to produce good work in order to receive good marks? Well, the principle remains the same. Whether you like your job or not, and whether you like doing some aspects of your job over others makes no difference; you still have to do it and you have to do it all and do it well.

Work is not nursery school; your manager is not there to beg you to do your job, nurse your feelings or be your motivational speaker. That is your job and nobody else's. A workplace is not a university; you do not get to decide what you want to do and when you will do it. If you have to do paperwork despite your great personality and passion for working with people over machines, you just have to stick it out and do it. No job is perfect and rosy; every job has both its perks and quirks.

It is very important to know that when it comes to your job, it is not just about your output but your attitude, especially when you have to do the not so favourite parts of your role. Simply put, how you do your job, i.e. your attitude towards your job, really says a lot about you. Refuse to allow your preferences to hinder and destroy your professional reputation. No company and absolutely no manager wants to work with a person who will only do great work when they feel like it, and not so great work when they lack passion for other aspects of their job.

The truth about work is that often you have to work even when you have zero inspiration. Only immature people wait for inspiration before they work. Imagine if we only worked when we felt like it? That may be never for some. In fact, it would be a disaster to rely on our feelings to do our jobs. Often we have to tell our bodies to shut up and work in order to get things done.

26

You must be willing to travel or relocate; the job of your dreams might not be in Johannesburg, Cape Town or Durban

Be willing to move

One day, I saw a CV of a 20-year-old that said she was not willing to relocate from Johannesburg. Now, maybe there were valid reasons for her reluctance to travel, such as a sick parent or maybe she was taking care of her siblings, but generally speaking, no 20-year-old should say that on their CV as it is very limiting. Why are we limiting ourselves so much?

As older people and members of society in general, we have to be careful what we say to these young souls. While we are on that, can we please stop telling 22-year-old girls, "God is going to give you a husband"! Give you a husband for what? How about, "Have you applied for that scholarship to Oxford, Harvard or Insead?" Or, "Did you hear about the R100 billion that the IDC has put aside to fund value-adding businesses?"

Back to my initial point, I was recently presenting a keynote address at the University of Limpopo and during several discussions with other people in the area, I had an 'aha' moment – a real awakening. There are serious business opportunities outside of Gauteng, so I must stop obsessing over the province. Your destiny and career are not tied to where you are currently located; be willing to move.

Reciprocal/Mutual support

Being nice costs nothing

One of the key problems we have in our country is that of entitlement. One of the biggest signs that you possess this exaggerated sense of self-worth/pride is when you expect others to support your hustle when you never support them, that is, if you preach but never allow yourself to be preached to. If you speak at conferences but you are never a delegate. If you expect colleagues to help you at work but you never help anyone. If you organise concerts but never attend other people's shows.

It is amazing how some people expect others to give that which they fail to. Just drop your 'prima donna' attitude and give that which you expect. When people come through for you, you have no idea what it takes and what they sacrifice to show up and support you; the least you can do is return the favour, whether they expect it or not. Indeed, we are aware of those of you who will only come through because you feel you owe us one, which lacks sincerity because nothing is more genuine and fulfilling than one who supports you simply because they can and want to. This is really just basic human courtesy; adopting such mannerisms seriously does no harm.

So my advice is... if a colleague is stuck and you know you can help, if you have to go an extra mile now and again just to help the other, if you can sacrifice (within limits of course) for the sake and benefit of the other, then by all means do so. You see, in the work environment there are very subtle and unwritten human relation rules. These rules are unspoken yet they have so much impact on how others treat you. You may not know it, but some of the reasons you may feel the world is against you at work may be because you gave people reasons to be against you.

You do not have to be a people pleaser and a yes-man/-woman, but simple acts of kindness and support for your colleagues will surely take you a long way. Remember the saying, 'You may forget how you treat people, but they will not forget how you treat them'. Well, it is true, so watch it! Being nice costs nothing but a smile, a helping hand and going the extra mile here and there, and giving it when someone least expects or demands it is priceless.

For those of you who take pride in being the mean boss, lighten up and let your hair down a bit. Be friendly and do your best to give what you can, because no man is an island and someday you will need the same or similar help. Everything you do counts for or against you. People keep tabs, just as you do, so the sooner you accept that you are not an exception to the rule, the better your relationships will be.

> *"A sense of entitlement is a cancerous thought process that is void of gratitude and can be deadly to relationships, businesses, and even nations."*
>
> (Steve Maraboli)[22]

28

Be nice to people and be helpful to colleagues – trust me, you will need them

Being nice only takes a priceless act of kindness

Every person you meet is a potential door to a new opportunity. This is the kind of attitude we should possess when we meet, relate and deal with people. I am not saying that we must reduce humanity to mere windows of opportunity, but we can easily forget the impact others may have on us, whether now or in the future. It is therefore necessary to adopt this mindset.

You never know where that cleaner may be in the future. You never know what your subordinate is capable of, and sometimes life will force you to need the people you think you may never need. So, remember to be nice and helpful even to those who do not deserve it; that kindness will go a long way. The point is to relate with everyone in such a manner that when the time comes, and trust me it always does, you can easily humble yourself and ask for help instead of requesting it shamefully and regrettably.

Being nice usually only takes a smile, a greeting, a sweet response, priceless acts of kindness and minor sacrifices from you. Sometimes our destinies are indeed tied to others and the truth is, the person you treat badly may be able to unlock your opportunities. You might not know it now because at this point you are at the top of the food chain and they are at the bottom, however I think at this age and point in time, we are all aware of how easily and quickly the wheel may turn and things may change.

29

Build your reputation

Your professional reputation is in your hands

Your reputation is one of the most significant elements that determine how people treat and relate to you. Interestingly though, reputation development is a slow process; it takes time to build and the building never really gets complete due to the continuous alterations.

I want you to realise in this chapter that you make or break yourself depending on the reputation you have built in the workplace. Ironically, we tend to think our reputations are beyond our control, when they are consciously formed, developed and transformed. Ever wondered why Peter could be known as a sweet somebody yet you know him as a harsh person? I bet you it is because your encounters with him have been quite harsh and thus it sounds crazy to you that Peter can be a sweetheart.

Your professional reputation is in your hands. Every little thing you do at work either enhances or diminishes your professional reputation. It is more what you do and less what you say that contributes to your reputation. My point here is this; whether you are aware of it or not, it is up to you which tasks you are given and trusted with at work, and why they are given and trusted to you. If you are perceived as the office player, the lazy bones, the complainer or the hard worker, it has all been by choice, whether consciously or unconsciously.

The sooner you realise and accept this, the better position you will be in to reclaim your authority, and to reshape and redesign your reputation. In a work environment, it is significant to be known as dependable, professional and cooperative. It always amazes me how certain people just do not get this. You acquire a reputation in your daily actions, outputs, behaviours, words and attitudes, so be mindful of how you portray yourself in this regard; it may just make or break you.

30

Avoid the 'We've always done it like this' brigade

Stay clear of people who suck every ounce of energy from you

In all organisations, there are those people I call the 'We've always done it like this' brigade. These are the people who have been there forever. Nothing moves or shakes them, nothing surprises them, and absolutely nothing inspires them anymore. They cannot be bothered by any of it – neither change nor innovation. Even change management solutions do not work on them. They think they know everything, to such an extent that they would not know a creative idea even if it were presented to them on a silver platter.

Again, we go back to the power of associations. These people will suck every ounce of energy from you; they will demotivate you and kill your enthusiasm, optimism and ambition. There is only one solution in dealing with them: avoid them at all costs!

31

Never hide behind an email address; no one promotes an anonymous person!

You have to be known in order to advance in your career

One day I was talking to a Human Resources consultant in a company of about 250 people. He mentioned to me that because they are a multinational company and highly technologically advanced, people often start working there without him knowing about it. The person's potential boss might be sitting in Dubai and therefore interviews are conducted through web-based tools. After confirming that the interviewee will be employed, she receives an employment contract and other on-boarding documents online. They then have to sign and upload them and someone based in India receives them.

The orientation process kicks in before the employee starts. She gets links to choose benefits and beneficiaries and regularly gets SMSes giving her directions, her direct manager's details, and all such information before her start day. Because of the nature of this business, he often finds out after a week or so that the new employee has started.

In organisations such as these, it is possible to bury yourself in your work and go about your business day in and day out, keeping to yourself. Whether it is by choice or circumstances, you can easily find that people do not actually know you beyond your email address. My friend, do not be tempted to be an email address. You are so much more than yourname@acompany.com. Dare to be visible and do not let the anonymity fool you, because you have to be known in order to be pushed, recommended and advanced in your career.

32

Width without depth will limit your career progression

Moderation is key in your career

In order to grow in your career, you need both career width and depth. In this context, width refers to gaining varied experiences from different disciplines and divisions, whereas depth refers to being an expert in what you do. I studied for both an MBA and an Executive Development Programme, which are both general management qualifications and were thus intended to give me width. These programmes offer a very superficial understanding of everything that happens in an organisation, and are therefore excellent for this purpose.

However, I am also a Human Resources/learning professional, and in my profession, and most probably yours as well, it is very important that I acquire depth. Many people do not stay long enough in a position to acquire the necessary depth. People work for a year or two and want out; they move on too quickly.

Do not get me wrong, I know I said people should not stay in one organisation forever, but it is important not to leave too early either – it is a balancing act. This is where it is important to practice the law of equilibrium, and, as Aristotle would say, the art of moderation. Moderation is key in your career my friend, whether you are sought after or you have proven yourself is not the point; the point is knowing when to leave and when to stay.

I think we all know that to learn and master anything in life requires consistent effort and practice. Read up on the 10,000 hours theory. According to Malcolm Gladwell, to excel in anything and achieve mastery, you must have done that particular thing for approximately 10,000 hours.[26] Do the maths and count how many days that is, and you will know how long it takes to master anything.

I think my point has been made thus far. You have to stay on that job to master it. That is why it is important to determine early on which career path you want to follow. I know it can be a long, daunting and confusing process, but the sooner you figure it out, the better. Do not be the man or woman who discovers their path on their 15th job in their 10th company within 20 years. Commit yourself to choosing your path, learning and empowering yourself in it, and eventually excelling there.

33

Taking offence easily will hinder your career progression

Being tough will always work to your advantage

Have you ever worked with people who are so fragile that you are afraid of giving them feedback? People need to toughen up a bit! I can guarantee that senior people in your organisation will offend you.

The relationship between offence and your career is generally linear. Offence leads to career regression; you will not go any further if people need to watch how and what they say to you. Whether it is destructive or constructive is not the point, you just have to take it and deal with it. Moreover, you not only have to take it, but you must receive it without an attitude or a dramatic verbal or non-verbal response.

You see, being tough in this regard will always work to your advantage, because if you are toughened up and not a cry-baby, there will be a maturity and seriousness about you, as well as a courage and wisdom portrayed and associated with you. You build a reputation and give a strong message about your character, that you cannot only take it, but you can handle it. Be known as that person and if it really cuts deep, because certain things have that power, then handle it on your own, keep it to yourself, or share it with your family and close friends.

34

Understand that work is an endless interview

People are always watching you

Yes, I said it; each and every day you spend at work is a continuous interview. Let me get this straight: you can arrive in the office as late as you can get away with, take the longest lunches, do as little as possible and leave as early as possible, but when you are being interviewed for a senior position in the organisation, you want to pull the "I'm willing to push beyond boundaries" card? What boundaries are you pushing beyond?

You may think nobody is watching or paying attention, but trust me, someone is; people are always watching you, every day and every moment. Act as if you have a stalker... watch your back, your words and your actions. Above all, watch your professional etiquette and mannerisms. Understand that you are in an interview all day, every day, forever.

The great thing about this interview, however, is that because of its endless nature, you have the opportunity to improve and change your responses every day. You know how after an interview you think of all the great responses you should have given? Well, this interview is such that you can give your best response the next day, or better yet, the next hour if you are not impressed with yourself!

The danger, however, is that because the interview is never ending, you can easily get too comfortable and thus fail to see what you need to improve or work on. With this chapter, I hope you have a daily reminder to be conscious of the interview without an exit door.

35

Do not give up on your dream

You will be tempted to think that your time will never come. It will.

Many South African football fans will know Itumeleng "Itu" Khune, the current goalkeeper and captain of both Kaizer Chiefs and our national football team, Bafana Bafana. The legendary soccer commentator, the late Cebo Manyaapelo, used to refer to Itu as "South Africa's number one". There are always arguments about whether Itu or Mamelodi Sundown's Denis Onyango is the best on the continent, which gives you an idea of how good Khune actually is. Yet many people forget that for many years, Itu was an understudy to the brilliant Brian "Spiderman" Baloyi at Kaizer Chiefs. Spiderman was so good that I suspect that at some point Itu thought he would never get a chance to play. If you are a corporate 'Itumeleng Khune' currently watching 'Brian "Spiderman" Baloyi' play, remember these things:

- You will be tempted to think that your time will never come. It will.
- You will doubt yourself a bit, thinking you will never reach Spiderman's standard. You will.
- You will feel some jealousy bubbling inside of you. Nip it in the bud.
- You may wish that Spiderman will have a career ending injury so that you get a chance. Do not. One day you will look back and wish to have just one more day with him. Embrace and enjoy the journey.
- You will be tempted to give up. Do not.
- When you go to EXCO to represent Spiderman once, you will do extremely well. Do not get carried away and think you are ready to take over. Everyone can be brilliant once. Spiderman has been doing this consistently for years, so calm down. Continue preparing.

Sometimes giving up may seem like the easiest thing to do, but you need to know this: if you are going to progress, you need to firmly entrench a 'no quit zone' in your mind – the type of mentality that says giving up is not an option! The only justifiable reason for quitting is if it is the wisest, rightest and best thing to do, not because it is an option, and certainly not because it is the easiest and least effortful way out.

I know life can really get hard sometimes; it can knock and push you way beyond what you think you can handle. Believe me when I say there have been days when giving up seemed to be the way to go, and I am certain that most of us have reached a point when things are just not coming together and our dreams feel too far-fetched and unrealistic. Sadly, a lot of people allow circumstances and these difficulties to convince them that they will never reach their goals. Moreover, they are convinced that the earlier they give in, the better off they are, as it would save them from hustles and embarrassments. South African local hip hop artist, Cassper Nyovest, attained one of his dreams when he became the first singer in South Africa to fill the 20,000-seater capacity stadium in Northgate, Johannesburg, without the help of an international act. What a moment that was. He did not stop there though; he went on to fill Orlando Stadium, FNB Stadium and almost filled Moses Mabhida stadium in Durban as well. What is your dream? Do not give up my friend.

A few years ago, I was attending a conference for people in the events industry and someone on stage said, “Every day, there are about 300 conferences in SA”. I was so frustrated by that statement as I thought to myself, “If there are 300 conferences each day in the country, then why am I only speaking once every two months?” My speaking engagements have become more frequent now; I am not where I should be, but I am definitely not where I was a few years ago either, and that is because I did not give up on my dream.

I strongly believe that if you cannot go through a day without thinking about your dream, giving up is absolutely not an option. It must mean that much to you to pursue it without restraint and never give in. Can you imagine where technology would be if Steve Jobs quit? Where the Virgin Group would be if Richard Branson gave up? The key point here is that all these great and life-changing achievements, trends and icons we now identify as successful were not birthed without struggle and temptations to quit.

36

Nobody will ever care about your development more than you; if you leave it in someone else's hands, it will not happen

You determine how far you go

Here is an interesting workplace fact: managers do care a bit about your development, but they care more about your performance. If you really want to advance in the organisation, understand this now: your development is your own baby.

Always initiate discussions with your manager about your development. Schedule a short meeting with your organisation's Head of Learning & Development for advice, volunteer to do other projects to learn; whatever it takes, just do it. It is your personal individual responsibility, so take it upon yourself and never expect anyone else to be concerned with your development except you. It is all in your hands my friend. You determine how far you go and the time it will take to get there.

Personal and Professional Development[27]

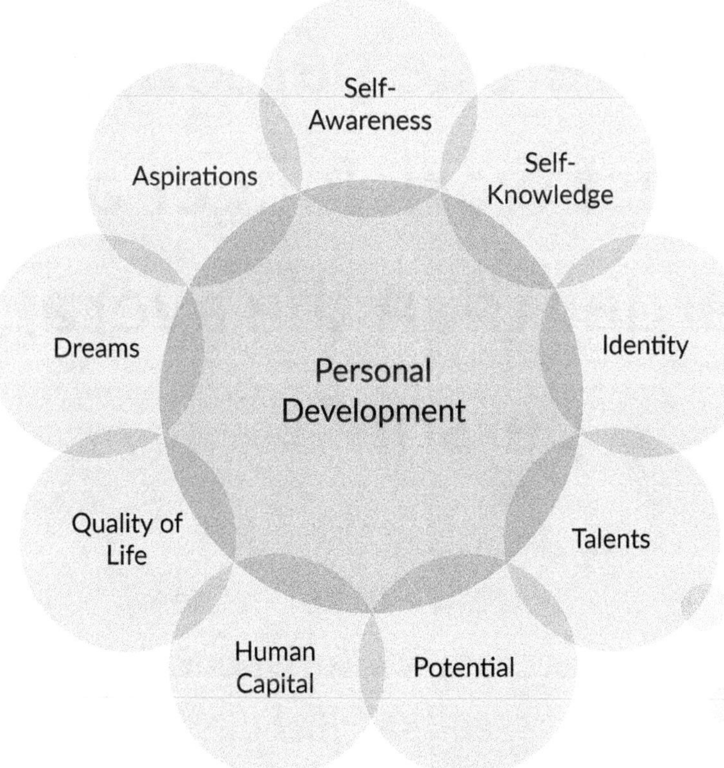

37

"To achieve more than an average person, you must work longer and harder than the average person" (Brian Tracy)[28]

You have to put in the necessary effort, hours and sacrifices

Many people do not actually realise how much you have to work to break into a different level in an organisation or move out of your economic/ social class. Many studies have proven that economic mobility is extremely difficult; the world system is designed to keep you in the same economic class you were born into. For example, if you were born into a working-class family and all you do every day is wake up, go to work, come back, watch TV and sleep, unfortunately you will most likely die in that class.

You have to seriously change your thinking, actions and habits in order to break into a different economic class. You have to be much more forceful and intentional about it. You have to put in the necessary effort, hours and sacrifices. Similarly, you ought to be more determined about breaking down the barriers that are impeding your progress. This means saying no to mediocrity and average performance. It means saying no to blending with the masses. It means choosing to add value and working harder and longer than the rest.

38

You must be allergic to some people at work; being seen with them will cost you the promotion you want

Avoid some people at all costs, simply because they will hinder your progress

Organisations have all kinds of people and personalities, which is what makes the work environment so dynamic and diverse. Some of us are naturally sociable and we like people, but in the work environment, not everyone can and should be your friend. There are some people who you should be allergic to, so you should avoid them at all costs, simply because they will hinder your progress.

I read an article written by Lolly Daskal, President and CEO of Lead From Within, who said that people who display the following symptoms are the kind you should avoid at work:[29]

1. **Toxic arrogance**

   There is a big difference between confidence and arrogance. Confidence inspires whereas arrogance intimidates. Arrogant people always think they know best and feel superior to others. They will never celebrate your confidence because it interferes with their arrogance.

2. **Toxic victimhood**

   Some of the most dangerous people you can have around you are the perpetual victims. These are people who look at their own issues and mistakes and always find others to blame. They lack accountability and will thus blame everyone else for their shortfalls, from their unloving parents to their current partners and ultimately you, whether as a friend or colleague. Toxic victims never take ownership of their mistakes and lives in general. It is always because someone else did 'this', which led him or her to doing 'that'. It is never just: "I did that, I made a mistake, I was wrong and I will face the consequences and resolve this."

3. **Toxic control**

   Controlling people know everything and the best way to do anything. However, they are usually very insecure beneath it all. The problem with hanging around the toxic controllers is that as long as they are around you, you will never get a chance to voice an idea or do anything yourself.

4. **Toxic envy**

   Those plagued with jealousy are never happy with what they have. Most of us keep them in our circles anyway, yet are surprised when they are not as happy as we thought they would be for us, our achievements and our successes. Our logic is that they may be envious, but they are our friends after all so we ought to expect them to rejoice with and for us.

   Can you really blame them though? I mean, if they are generally discontented and unhappy with whatever they have and wherever they are, how do you expect them to be happy when good things happen to you? They simply lack that ability; they cannot appreciate it when others achieve or move forward. They often feel that if anything good is going to happen, it should happen to them. They are the 'cream of the crop' and only they deserve the best, after all.

5. **Toxic liars**

   As long as there are people, there will be liars. Chronic liars are harmful because you never know what to believe, so you cannot count on their word nor their promises. They will lie to you about others and thus lie to others about you; it is what it is.

6. **Toxic negativity**

   You probably know someone who is always angry, resentful and suspicious of everything. Negativity destroys relationships and spending time with negative people will make you feel like they are sucking the life out of you. For peace and progress' sake, stay away!

7. **Toxic greed**

   So much of our culture tells us to want more, achieve more and earn more. To a certain degree, that kind of desire and ambition can be good, but it becomes problematic when 'wanting' becomes toxic. This is because when toxic people want something, they want it all – that which is theirs and that which is not alike. Moreover, when they have anything in abundance, rather than doing or being kind to others, the focus is solely on themselves and their lives.

8. **Toxic judgment**

   There is a big difference between making a judgment and being judgmental. Judgments are objective and based on discernment, whereas being judgmental is about criticism. Judgmental people are always quick to jump to conclusions; they are poor listeners and communicators.

9. **Toxic gossip**

   Gossipers see themselves as having a deep conversation about someone; an exchange of information. They do it to elevate themselves above their insecurity and there is no distinction between speculation and fact. Few things are more destructive than gossip. Talking about others will never change nor improve anything about yourself or your circumstances. If anything, the more you gossip, the more critical and harsher you become, which hinders you from learning from others and allowing yourself to grow as a result.

10. **Toxic lack of character**

    When someone lacks integrity and honesty, that is, when cheating, lying, manipulating, gossiping and greed are part of the norm, there are few things these people will not do to get their way. If they decide you are an obstacle to them, they will come after you with everything they have. Be careful of people who have few barriers and lack a conscience… they will destroy you.

39

Stop your obsession with having fun; fun will limit your progress

Navigate back to where you ought to be

For some of us, the reason we do not see progress in our lives is simple: we are just more committed to having fun than to our own development. I mean, seriously, it is not compulsory to go clubbing every weekend, going out to chill and hanging out just for fun, attending concerts, watching movies and whatever else we do for fun. Sometimes you just need to sit yourself down and do that assignment or research you have been threatening to do. An obsession with fun will hinder your progress.

When South Africa's DJ Shimza and Dr Malinga wrote the song with the line: *"Akulalwa; si jaiva ubusuku bonke"*, meaning "We don't sleep, we party all night long", we must contrarily say *"Akulalwa; sisebenza ubusuku bonke"*, meaning "We don't sleep; we work all night long". I am not criticising these artists or their song – their work ethic is actually quite exemplary. I am merely using this to challenge those of us who spend 80% of our time partying and chilling, and then wonder why we never progress.

If you have time for everything else except the tasks that you should do, then sooner or later, fun becomes the norm and fun is all that you are about; it literally encompasses everything about you. Please do not become that person! Refuse to be about that life; it is not worth it – not when you have so much potential and such big dreams.

You cannot afford to compromise yourself, your ambitions and your destiny like that. Refuse to be the person everyone knows to call when they are bored or want something to do because they know you are always game for anything. If you need to grow a backbone, grow it in this area. You cannot be a yes-man/-woman in this regard – be disciplined. Know your priorities and set them; let them be known and stick to them without compromise.

Fun is necessary, yes, but fun cannot be the most predominant element of our lives – not if we want to get ahead and progress in this life. If progress is what we want then fun is an element worth compromising now and again. Remember, progress requires effort, determination and sacrifice, so let us be realistic. What is a bit of fun compared to the results we will reap if we fully apply ourselves, commit to our personal development, and utilise our utmost potential?

I believe it will be worthwhile so think long-term. Most of us lose out on significant valuable time because when it comes to fun, our thinking is like a short circuit.

Here are three significant truths about fun to remember before choosing fun over work:

1. There is something called too much fun.
2. Fun never runs out; it will always be there.
3. You can never exhaust fun – it only exhausts you. This is because fun often compromises our rest, and ultimately, exhaustion hampers our performance and functioning even days after the few hours of fun that we had.

Consider this a warning: if you continue with this 'fun over work' mentality and lifestyle, if you continue playing more than you work, if your 80/20 rule means 80% fun and 20% work, then trust me, poverty will attack you like an armed robber!

Please do not get me wrong. I am not saying we must lead boring and *fun-less* lives because we are only concerned with our progress. On the contrary, we need some thrill and excitement or we will quickly exhaust ourselves and get burnt out, so I am not suggesting that you do that to yourself. I am merely saying we must watch how much of our time, resources, lives, and ultimately ourselves, we give to fun.

Some of you were supposed to be managers, directors and CEOs by now. You were supposed to have your companies up and running, be featured on *Forbes* magazine and be guests on popular radio and TV shows, but your obsession with fun keeps obstructing your progress.

Let us re-evaluate our standpoint regarding what fun means and how much fun we can afford to have. If you are honest enough with and to yourself, and realise that you have been off track and side-tracked by fun, then it is time to reroute my friend. Change your current location and navigate back to where you ought to be and find your way back to progress.

40

People judge you harshly when you are untested, it is not personal; focus on the work and MOST will come around

Keep quiet, work hard, prove yourself

When I wrote *Bulls & Bears: Life lessons from the financial markets*, I mentioned this point. When former President Thabo Mbeki was inaugurated as president in 1999, the Rand fell to over R6 to the dollar for the first time (it is hard to believe but the Rand was averaging about R3.50 to the dollar in 1994). The Rand fell even further when Tito Mboweni was appointed Governor of the South African Reserve Bank. Is it not interesting that the same people who were nervous when Thabo Mbeki was elected president and Tito Mboweni was appointed governor are now praising both men for fiscal discipline?

Those who were nervous are now their biggest fans. It was so fascinating to see the market's response when Minister Tito Mboweni was announced as Finance Minister after the resignation of Minister Nhlanhla Nene on 10 October 2018. Most commentators said he was a "safe pair of hands". That was not what they said when he was appointed governor years ago. This is the same thing that will happen with you when you get a new role. People will get nervous; they will criticise you and some will not give you the support you need and deserve. This is normal and has very little to do with you as a person. Keep quiet, work hard, prove yourself and you will see those who were your critics turn into major fans.

Let the analysts talk while you focus on the work at hand; focusing on the noise will limit your progress

Focus on the work and people will come around

It was September 2011 when the then South African President, Jacob Zuma, introduced the nation to the new Chief Justice of South Africa, The Honourable Justice Mogoeng Mogoeng. Before that, Chief Justice Mogoeng had been a judge of the Constitutional Court for two years, Judge President of the North West High Court for five years, and had many years of judicial experience. Despite this experience, when he was appointed many people questioned his capabilities. He was under so much scrutiny it seemed unfair. Do not focus on the noise. Focus on the work and people will come around.

Circle of Concern vs. Circle of Control[30]

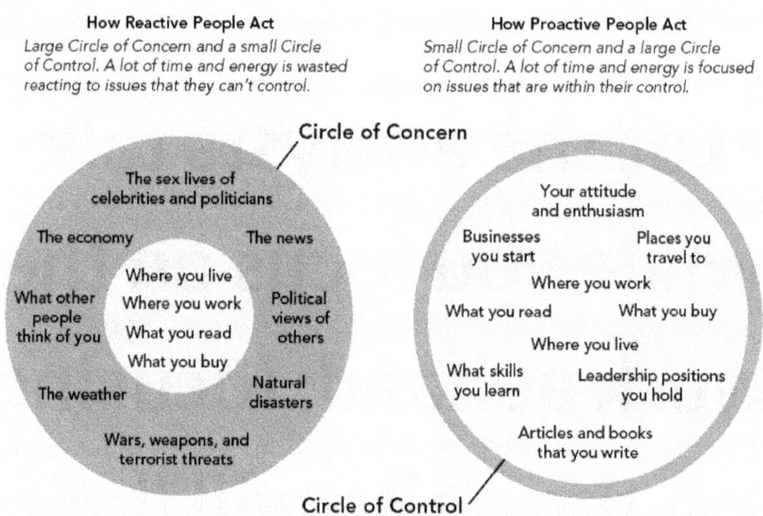

Do not let anyone make you feel you are less ambitious if you want to climb the corporate ladder instead of starting your own business

Work with, not against your career anchor

It is a well-known fact that South Africa has a very poor entrepreneurial culture and I understand that we need to change that. However, it appears that the predominant method used to encourage this change has been to imply that people who want to work in corporate SA are boring and that they lack ambition and determination in life. We must not create an impression that having a corporate job is boring; that people who work in corporates lack ambition and initiative. We need strong people in corporate SA as well, so if you know that this running your own business thing is not for you, please do not feel pressured to start one. Enjoy your corporate career to the fullest. The money is good, as are your opportunities for progress; I used to work in HR, so I know.

When I teach career development, I always spend time talking about career anchors. We all have different career anchors – that one element in a person's career that he or she will not give up, even in the face of difficult choices. If you cannot imagine yourself going back to full-time employment even in the face of difficulty, it is probably because autonomy/independence is your career anchor. If you cannot imagine the possibility that you might not have a salary for a month or two or three, security/stability is probably your anchor. When you build a career ignoring your anchor, turmoil becomes the order of the day. It is always better to work with, not against your career anchor.

43

Money does matter

All you need is to find your sweet spot

Do not make the mistake of listening to the "Money doesn't matter; just follow your passion" crowd. I have studied a lot of models on assessing one's strengths and choosing a career, and I still think Jim Collins' model is one of the best as it is much more comprehensive, realistic and practical than most. He calls it the 'Hedgehog Concept'. This concept is based on an ancient Greek parable that states: "The fox knows many things, but the hedgehog knows one big thing." In the parable, the fox uses many strategies to try to catch the hedgehog. It sneaks, pounces, races and plays dead, yet every time it walks away defeated, its tender nose pricked by spines. The fox never learns that the hedgehog knows how to do one big thing perfectly: **defend itself**.[31, 32]

A business researcher and consultant, Jim Collins developed the idea in his classic 2001 book, *Good to Great.* In it, Collins argued that organisations will more likely succeed if they can identify the one thing that they do best – their Hedgehog Concept. This simple, crystalline concept flows from a deep understanding about the intersection of three circles: 1) what you are deeply passionate about; 2) what you can be the best in the world at; and 3) what best drives your economic or resource engine.[33]

The Personal Hedgehog

According to Collins, "The concept of the three circles, or the Hedgehog Concept, is powerful for not only corporations and non-profits and organizations, but also individuals. Imagine you were able to get or construct work for yourself that meets three tests: you're passionate about it and you love to do it; you're genetically encoded for it, so that when you do it you just feel like you were born to do it; and finally, you're able to make the economics in your life work—you get well paid for it or perhaps there's some other way of funding it with an economic engine".[34]

The significant questions to ask yourself are these:

1. What am I passionate about? What do I love to do?

2. What am I genetically encoded for? What feels right when I do it?

3. What can I get paid for?

By answering these, you will know if you are engaged in work that fits your own three circles.

Here is the good news. You do not have to choose between these three, and all you need is to find your sweet spot.

The Hedgehog Concept[35]

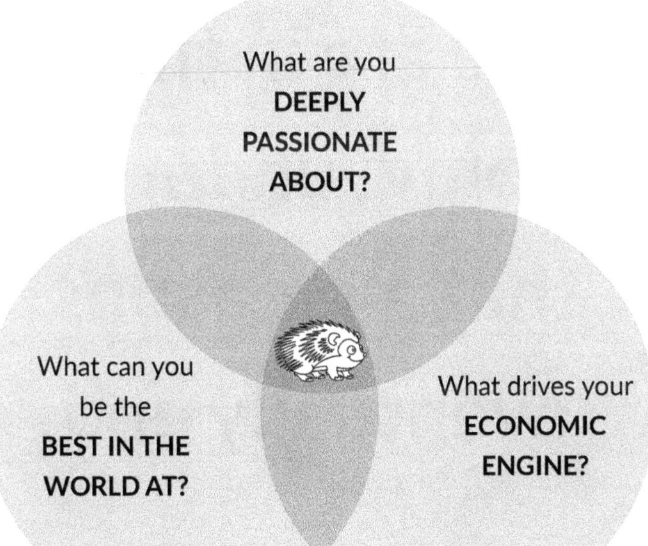

If you are in the 'gig economy', understand that all seasons eventually end

Embrace all seasons alike

The gig economy is basically the freelancing economy. These are people who work for different employers without any exclusivity rights. There was a time when this was a terrain for artists and professional speakers like me, but the dynamic nature of employment has led to more and more people opting to be freelancers.

If you are in the 'gig economy' then you will know that there are seasons when nobody wants to invite you to sing, speak or whatever else you do. Do not doubt your gift because of a dry season; a lack of rain does not mean that you are a bad farmer, and all seasons eventually end. Likewise, there will be times when you are flourishing and the star of the company or your manager's favourite, but there will also be a time when you are just doing okay or even not so well. Embrace all seasons alike; they all eventually end and alternate, after all.

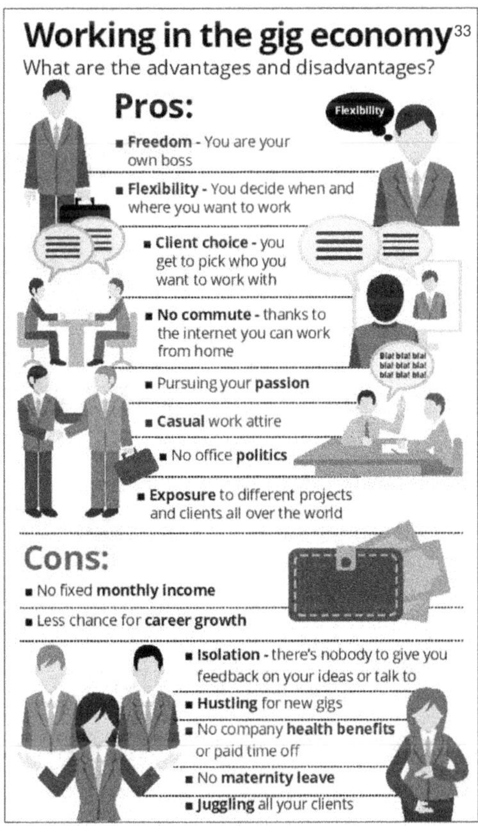

Expand your thinking; deal with the limitations in your mind

No more tiny little dreams – think global

On Friday 11 September 2015, I achieved something very significant. You see, up until then, I had never set foot in a Lamborghini dealership. I had always been very afraid to do it and I often questioned if I was worthy enough to enter one. But that Friday, on my way to a meeting, I decided to sign in (yes, you sign in) at the Lamborghini and Bentley dealership on William Nicol Drive in Bryanston, Johannesburg, and confidently walked onto the floor and viewed those machines in close proximity.

I made a serious shift in mind-set that day. This is how it all starts, after all. I still do not own a Lamborghini, but finally I can actually imagine owning one. This is the shift that we all need to make in order to progress in life. Deal with the limitations in your own mind. Can you imagine being in the top ten percent of the people in your field? Can you comprehend being the most senior accountant in your company? Can you comprehend being a partner at one of the big five auditing firms in the world?

Recently, I watched a TED Talk by someone I grew up with, Dr Patience Mthunzi, who is a senior researcher at the Human Sciences Research Council. She is currently spearheading global research on the ability to cure HIV with lasers. From her beginnings on the dusty streets of Soweto, she is now recognised globally for her work. It is possible.

A South African company such as Aspen Holdings also inspires me in this manner. It started in South Africa and became so global that currently, less than 25% of its earnings come from SA. Aspen is now a supplier of branded and generic pharmaceuticals and nutritional products in more than 150 countries across the world. They have selected their territories and are dominating them. They might be going through a rough patch right now, but I still believe in the fundamentals of this business.

My thinking has become global as well. No more tiny little dreams of opening a *spaza* shop. I think global now. Can you imagine it? Change your thinking!

"If you put yourself in a position where you have to stretch outside your comfort zone, then you are forced to expand your consciousness."

(Les Brown)[37]

After you change your thinking, have a work ethic to match it

All you need is a healthy work ethic and discipline

In the previous point, I asked if you could imagine being in the top ten percent of people in your field. An interesting and noteworthy point about people who are in the top ten percent of their field is that after they have put in all that work, they do not go out and celebrate – they continue to work.

I was thinking about this recently after I attended a conference of professional speakers in Washington, D.C. People who are at the top of their game had surrounded me; when I got back home, I was slightly frustrated. All of us want to be around successful people, but often hanging around with people on top of their game can be very discouraging.

You start to realise that the reason you do not operate at that level is not racism, favouritism, nepotism or any other 'isms'. The reason is YOU. That is obviously frustrating because it is much easier to blame the 'isms' and much harder to admit that YOU are the problem. You have a weak work ethic; you are not disciplined enough; you have too many excuses; and and and! You see, if you are going to progress, you have to modify and fine-tune your work ethic.

I laughed very hard recently when I was emceeing the National Talent Management Conference and one of the speakers, Dr Marko Saravanja, the Chairman of Regenesys Business School, said, "You don't have to be intelligent to get a PhD; believe me, I have one". He made the point that all you really need is a healthy work ethic and discipline.

I prepare most of my speeches and do most of my writing at three o'clock in the morning, for example. When most people wake up, I am already about three hours ahead. Create a work ethic that will not only match, but also sustain and continuously improve, your role and position.

Prepare for linear career progression but leave some room for exponentiality

Never overlook nor undermine the spiritual element to career progression

Often, as human beings, we tend to think that our career progression will be linear, progressing from one stage to another in a single series of steps. In other words, I will be an Agent, then a Team Leader, then a Manager – or whichever order applies to your industry.

Believe it or not, there is a component of faith in this progression thing. It is important to believe that you can skip some steps in your progression and still be able to handle it. Prepare for linear progression, but leave space for exponentiality. I know we all have different beliefs, but never overlook nor undermine the spiritual element to career progression.

Career progression plan example

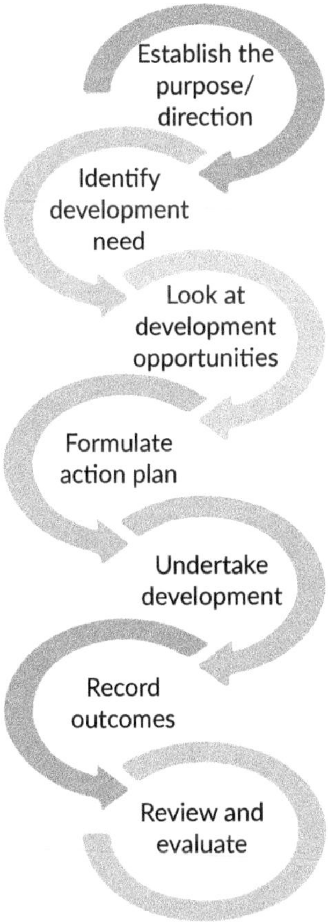

Establish the purpose/ direction

Identify development need

Look at development opportunities

Formulate action plan

Undertake development

Record outcomes

Review and evaluate

48

Relentless preparation will cause you to be seen next to the best in the world

What you do in obscurity will eventually bring you to the spotlight

Until 27 August 2015, many South Africans (including me) did not know who Anaso Jobondwana was. Then, in what seemed to be all of a sudden, out of nowhere, we woke up to that iconic picture of Jobondwana running next to Usain Bolt during the 15th IAAF World Championships at the National Stadium in Beijing, China.

I say it seemed all of a sudden because to us, it seemed that way. For Jobondwana, however, who had been preparing for that moment in obscurity, it was not sudden at all. Relentless preparation will allow you to be seen next to the best in the world. As you continue to work hard in obscurity, keep your determination and persistence. Nobody might know you and no one may want to give you a chance, BUT, one day you will appear next to the best in the world and everyone will ask: "Where did he come from?" Just like Johnnie Walker, keep going because your time will surely come. What you do in obscurity will eventually bring you to the spotlight.

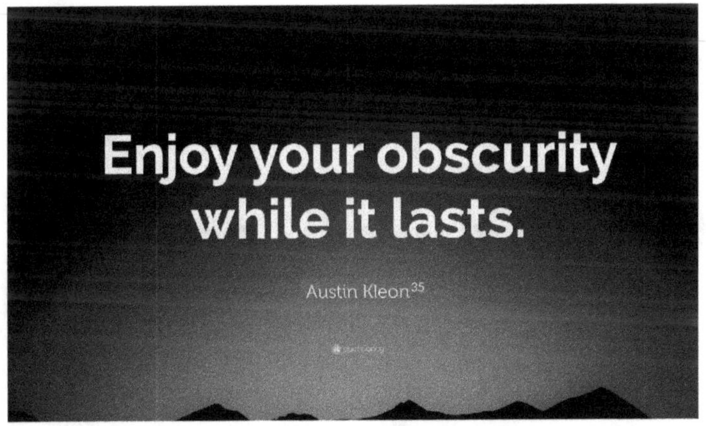

49

Your opportunity will surely come

When opportunity comes, it is too late to prepare, so start now

Sometimes it may seem like everyone else is being promoted and advancing in his or her career except you. At such times, you need to be reminded that your opportunity will surely come. It may be delayed, but eventually it will come into being. Keep doing the right things and mixing the right ingredients: plan, prepare and work hard, and it will surely come.

There was an organisation that always asked me to quote them to facilitate workshops for them, but never gave me the opportunity. A friend of mine asked me why I continued to quote them, as they were just using me to comply with their 'three quotes requirement'. I told him that I was aware that they just wanted to get three quotes, and I was also aware that they had their favourite facilitator. What I also knew, however, is that one day their favourite facilitator would be unavailable and they would have to use me. I was like a goalkeeper patiently waiting for his chance, I said to him. About two months ago, it actually happened; they asked me to speak at one of their conferences. I was so emotional when it happened, remembering what I had told my friend.

I put my all into that speech; in my subconscious, I wanted them to forget their favourite. I have done more business with that company now. Your opportunity will come. I have asked this question and I will ask it again: will you be ready when it comes? Remember that preparation comes before the presented opportunity. When opportunity comes, it is too late to prepare, so start now.

50

Do you want to know who is responsible for the lack of progress in your life? Look in the mirror...

Sometimes we have to look in the mirror before we blame others

"An important decision I once made was to resist playing the Blame Game. The day I realized that I am in charge of how I will approach problems in my life, that things will turn out better or worse because of me and nobody else, that was the day I knew I would be a happier and healthier person. And that was the day I knew I could truly build a life that matters."

(Steve Goodier)[39]

"The problem is NOT funding; the problem is me." I came to this conclusion in 2004 when I was running my first business, Amakhono Esizwe. I submitted my business plan to a few development finance institutions and they all declined my application. I cried racism. I cried corruption. I blamed everything and everyone else until one day, I saw a business plan of someone who was actually funded and at that point I realised that the problem was not 'out there', but within me.

I saw what a quality business plan looked like and to be honest, mine was sloppy. Sometimes we have to look in the mirror before we blame everyone and everything else; the answer is often closer to us than we think.

"Blaming others is an act of refusing to take responsibility. When a person can't accept the fact or the reality, they blame another person or the situation instead of taking accountability."

(Dee Dee Atner)[40]

"Blame doesn't empower you. It keeps you stuck in a place you don't want to be because you don't want to make the temporary, but painful, decision to be responsible for the outcome of your own life's happiness."

(Shannon L. Alder)[41]

51

Study the language that has weight and speak it

Speaking your organisation's language will propel your progress

In every organisation, there is a language that has weight. I spent a big portion of my adult life working in banks and I realised very early that if you want to catch the attention of executives in a bank, you have to understand "bank speak". I was fortunate enough to be chosen to study an international certificate in retail banking, and after that, how senior people viewed me changed because I could speak their language. Find out which language carries weight in your organisation and learn it fast; it will propel your progress.

"Once you desire progress more than convenience, obstacles no longer stop but propel you."

Benjamin P. Hardy[42]

52

Learn to mind your own business

Never give anyone ammunition against yourself

If I ever had to choose one mantra to live by, it would be this: make it your ambition to lead a quiet life, to mind your own business, and to work with your own hands. Many people care too much about other people's business and neglect their own.

When you are at work, please remember that you are there for yourself and not anyone else. Stay out of office dramas and if possible, avoid office politics and office romances – most never end well. Most importantly, though, do not be the cause of the drama and politics by sticking your nose in where it does not belong.

In minding your own business, you can teach others to mind their own too. Remember, at the end of the day, work is work; it is important to maintain professionalism in how you carry yourself, and most importantly, in your speech, attitude and actions. Make it your mission to watch what you say, how you say it, and who you say it to. Unfortunately, some people will stop at nothing to get ahead, even if it means disclosing personal information to bad-mouth, sabotage and ruin your reputation.

It is also very important to remember that such disclosure may be done deliberately or unconsciously, as some people may share your personal information for the right reasons, but unfortunately to the wrong person. It is therefore important to keep your business to yourself, especially that which puts you in a professionally vulnerable position. These are cases in which your performance and chances for a promotion may be negatively affected. The answer is to never give anyone ammunition against yourself; be very careful who you open up to and the details you disclose.

53

We all need inspiration – find something or someone that inspires you

Open your heart and you will receive inspiration

I do not want to get into religion because this book is for everyone, but I have to tell you a story that was a great inspiration to me.

I think it was Sunday, 13 February 2005. Our church landlord at the community hall in Orange Farm Extension 2 had told us that we could not use the hall that day, so we were using a smaller, shoddier hall and combined it with a tent to hold our Sunday service. It was raining, the roof was leaking and the mood was a bit sombre, as you can imagine.

Our then Pastor, who is also my role model, mentor and inspiration, arrived. As he was about to begin preaching, someone made an announcement that our Pastor had just received his PhD, which would be conferred on him soon. Before that moment, I had never known anyone with a PhD. Suddenly, the mood changed. Suddenly, many of us believed it was possible. That moment changed my life.

We all need some inspiration, and most of the time, it is right in front of our noses and we need not look any further. Someone does not have to be older than you or famous to inspire you; I have received inspiration from those my age and younger alike. If you open your heart to it, you will receive that inspiration, whichever form it comes in.

54

Ignoring the invisible fences

There is NO fence, there is NO boundary and there is NO limit; cross OVER

A pet fence or fenceless boundary is an electronic system designed to keep a pet or other domestic animals within a set of predefined boundaries without the use of a 'real or physical fence'. A mild electronic shock is delivered as and when the pet tries to cross the boundary. The pet soon learns to avoid the invisible fence location, making it an effective virtual barrier. In psychological learning theories the fence is a stimulus that elicits a response, which in time becomes so reinforced that it is unconsciously elicited.

Unfortunately, as human beings, we also suffer from the Invisible Fence Syndrome (IFS). (I just invented a psychological disorder that may someday make it to the *Diagnostic and Statistical Manual of Mental Disorders*!) But let me move on to elaborate how the IFS works. The key symptom is giving up based on past experience. The invisible fence exists because every time you try to do something and fail, you start believing there is a boundary and that you must not attempt to break it if you want to avoid negative feedback. Ultimately, you learn that you should not try because the chances are you will not succeed.

Some of you have applied so many times for a position that you do not even want to try anymore. Let me share the good news; the key fact about learning is that we can both learn and unlearn. Therefore, because we can learn to stop trying to cross a boundary, we can also unlearn this, and then *relearn* to keep trying until we make it. Today I would like to say to you, there is NO fence, there is NO boundary and there is NO limit. Cross OVER my friend. Try again. Go for it!

55

Understand that others will try to hinder your progress – toughen up

In a work environment, relationships play out a bit differently

Some people enter the workplace with a very naïve mentality, believing that everyone cares about them, their issues and their successes. As a result, they tend to open up and trust a bit too much, sometimes to the wrong person or crowd. Unfortunately, this naïve mindset is delusional and may hamper your career progress and success.

The fact is this... in a work environment, relationships play out a bit differently. Work is not home and your colleagues are not really your family or friends. For this reason, not everyone has your best interests at heart, and not everyone will look out for you and want you to get ahead.

In fact, people, both friends and enemies, or rather 'frenemies', will try to sabotage and block your progress. They will bad-mouth you, jeopardise your work and even misrepresent you. It may look like they are succeeding for a while but NO ONE can block your progress permanently. NO ONE!

The best you can do is toughen up and snap out of your naïvety. Understand and accept that you just have to trust and rely on yourself more. I am not suggesting that you possess a 'me against the world' kind of attitude, because some people genuinely care and want what is best for you. I am just saying you must be tough enough to realise that some people can be a wolf in sheep's clothing, and it is your responsibility to protect yourself and stay away from them.

When they eventually reveal themselves to you, do not allow yourself to hate, feel resentful or be bitter. Merely understand that it is just part of life and work, so be courageous and tough enough to walk away in peace and avoid vengeance.

56

Have bias for action

Have a personal vision and then ACT

“I thought about it first” is the language of regret. Do not regret sitting on your idea without putting action to it. Be known as a person who does things and not one who talks about things. As Benjamin Franklin commented, “Well done is much better than well said”. There is a popular English proverb that says, “One of these days is none of these days”. Do not be the type of person who says, “I will do it one of these days”. Just do it! I often say that there are requirements to any change – be dissatisfied with where you are, have a personal vision and then ACT.

57

Be the cream of the crop in your field

Do not be a once-off hard worker – work hard all the time

There is not really much I can add to make this point. To set yourself up for career progression and advancement simply means you ought to do your best all the time. The difference between the cream of the crop and the masses simply lies in the fact that what the cream of the crop do every day is what the masses do once in a while. So do not be a once-off hard worker – work hard all the time. This does not mean you must be at work from 8am to 8pm all day, every day; you still need a life!

The point is to establish yourself as someone who excels in all they do, no matter how small or insignificant a task may seem. Be known as the go-to-person when excellence and the best results are required. Are you one of the best in your field? How do you know? Have you done an objective assessment? May I suggest that you perform your own personal SWOT (Strengths, Weaknesses, Opportunities and Threats) analysis?[43]

Personal Career SWOT Analysis. Ask yourself the following questions...

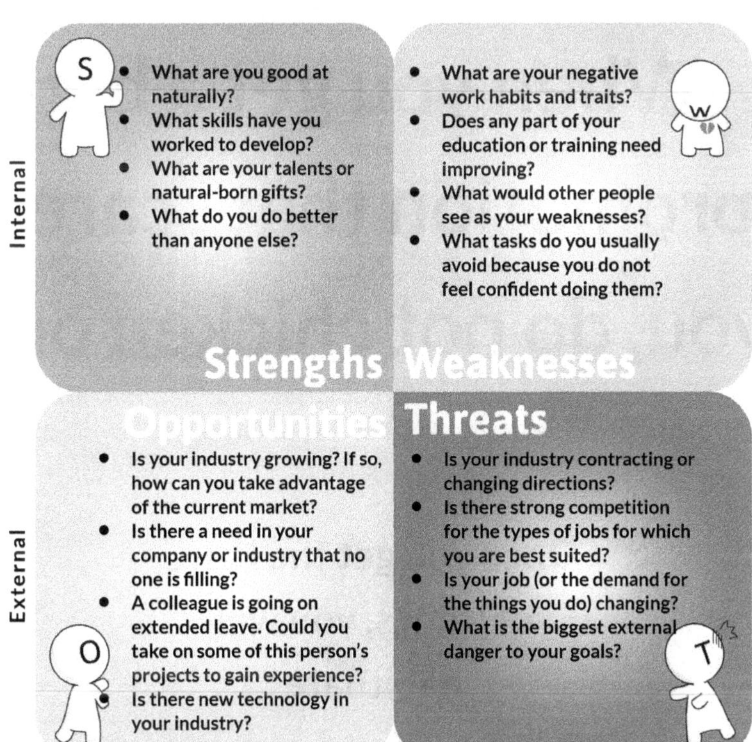

58

When you get a big promotion that scares you, do not chicken out

Once you get the hang of things, you will habituate

Promotions are frightening, particularly if you have been an exceptional performer at your current level. You are used to being the star and all of a sudden, you are not fully performing because you are new. It may be tempting to tell your boss that you want your old job back; in fact it is normal to feel like that, but do not chicken out – it will be much better in a few months' time!

There is a psychological concept called 'habituation', which is a phenomenon that can be used in a swimming analogy. When you get into the swimming pool for the first time on any day the water may feel very cold, but several minutes later, you have adapted and it feels okay – normal even. Likewise, your new role may be a bit scary, overwhelming and challenging at first, but once you get the hang of things, you will habituate and get used to it. Do not be so hard on yourself; all in good time, my friend.

59

Schedule time in your diary to think about your career development

Whatever is scheduled will be done

Whatever is scheduled will be done. If you keep thinking about how you need to think about your career development, but never make time to actually think about it and plan, then you are as good as the employee who wastes time on social media, idle chit-chat with colleagues, and other unnecessary time-wasters when they have a deadline coming up. They will keep finding excuses and justifying their actions, and never really get to the work until it is too late and the pressure is too high.

Never allow pressure to force you to stop thinking and planning for your career development. It is better to start thinking of it now before it becomes a must, because when it becomes a necessity, then you know you are not in a good place. Think and plan in advance; make the time because nobody will make it for you, nor will anyone think about your own development on your behalf.

Do not compromise your Continuous Professional Development (CPD)

Never settle or think you have reached your peak

Continuous professional development simply means consistent and non-stop learning and self-enhancement in your career and industry. It means you are devoted to improving your knowledge and skills; that you are open to innovation and implementing new strategies, systems and processes to keep up with the times. Who would want to be operated on by a surgeon who last developed himself in 1981? Nobody!

Refuse to be irrelevant and out-dated. Keep current. Stay on top of your game. Read up on industry research and current trends, and commit yourself to implementation. Never settle or think you have reached your peak, because wherever you are, there is always an opportunity to learn, grow and fully apply yourself. You never reach your destination until you die.

Improve your education/skills

It is never too late to learn and enhance yourself

A school of thought has emerged which claims that education is not important because we can succeed without it. Proponents of this argument often tell us about people such as Steve Jobs and Bill Gates. I do not think these people are wrong, but context really matters in this instance, and in South Africa, education definitely matters. It is very clear that in South Africa, there is a correlation between people's education levels and their economic mobility.

After analysing household data from 2000 to 2007, Branson, Leibbrandt and Zuzu established clear, positive links between further study and access to the labour market.[44] Their findings showed that having a matric qualification increased the likelihood of formal employment compared to qualifications lower than a matric. Moreover, compared to the group with less than a matric certificate, obtaining a tertiary qualification improved the likelihood of formal employment up to three times. Education matters, so if you have a chance to improve yours, do it.

You may be in a comfortable job with a great salary, and whether you went to school or not is beside the point. The point is that wherever you are, whatever your academic history and however you got that job, it is never too late to learn and enhance yourself.

You may be doing your job well and know all you think there is to know about it, but trust me, you can never know enough, so do not close yourself off from learning. It does not have to be an intense full-on qualification; taking short classes to enhance yourself, develop your skill set and be informed about your industry and work role will never do you any harm. Try it and see for yourself. It will do you wonders and intensify your interest.

62

Develop a career plan

Width is great but depth is an absolute necessity to your career

This sounds very fluffy but it is absolutely critical. Allow me to share with you my career plan, which I developed in 2011 as a guideline. As with most things it has changed over the years, but it is still a useful guide:

Career Plan 2011-2021 (10-year plan)			
Year	**Age**	**Position**	**Skills to Learn**
2021	40 +	CEO of my own people development company and full-time speaker	Professional Speaking
2018-2021 (3 years)	38-40	Group HR Director in financial services or engineering company	Executive Education
2016-2018 (3 years)	35-38	Chief Learning Officer in financial services or engineering company	Executive Education Relationships
2013-2015 (3 years)	32-34	EXCO level role (Head of Cluster/Segment L&D in a bank or Head of Divisional HR)	HR Practices Study Talent Management & Labour Law
2011-2012 (2 years)	30-31	Snr. Manager: Learning & Development	Current Position

After I wrote this, I left corporate South Africa earlier than I had planned in order to pursue my vision of being a full-time professional speaker and entrepreneur. You may need tweaks here and there, but having a flexible guideline is always better than no guideline at all. A guideline will serve as a constant reminder for your desired outcome and keep you on track instead of allowing yourself to be swayed and blown by every passing wind.

If you are young and reading this book, consider yourself blessed because you have an impactful tool. One of the reasons I am actually writing this book is for you, young person, because I wish I had a manual like this when

I was younger. I am thus honoured to present this to you and hope that it inspires you to structure your career and progression goals.

The thing about being young is that most of you prefer going with the flow and just taking things as they come, which is okay, but unfortunately that can be a disadvantage in your career. Most of you tend to just enter the workplace without a clear vision and career plan, which is understandable as universities do not teach this. Now that you have the knowledge, however, use it.

Find out what you want and where you want to be, then plan how to get there so that you do not unnecessarily find yourself in 10 different jobs within 10 different companies in a very few years. As I mentioned earlier, width is great but depth is an absolute necessity to your career progression, especially if you aim to be in the corporate sector for a long time and want to be in a senior managerial position that pays you a high-end salary.

Four steps to effective career planning[45]

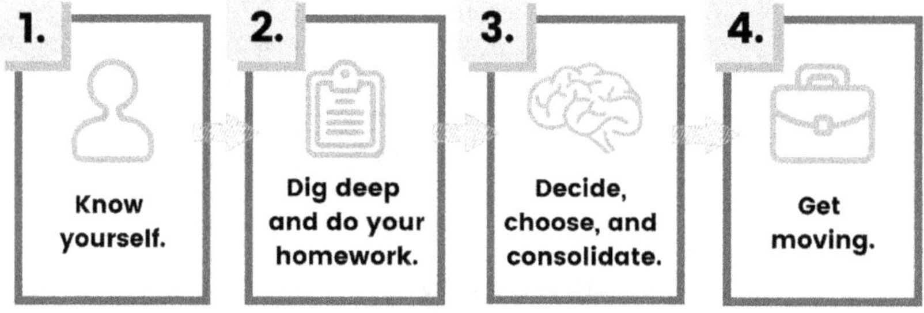

63

Do not let your career goals be a secret – talk to your boss about them

Chances are that he/she will have the ability to make them happen

When I knew that I wanted to be a professional speaker, I spoke to my then boss about it. That was one of the best decisions I have ever made. Knowing that I am a good performer, she allowed me to speak at a very small meeting with some of our team leaders. The title of my talk was 'Help; I'm a team leader!'

After that talk, she received feedback that I added so much value that she asked me to draft a proposal, which was to be sent to EXCO, for me to present motivational talks for all staff members in our division. That, ladies and gentlemen, launched my professional speaking career. Every time I tell her that she played a major role in my speaking career, she brushes me off, but I know as well as I know my name that she did, and I am eternally grateful.

I know some bosses will not support you like my boss supported me. Maybe they will not go to the same lengths, but please talk to your boss about your career ambitions in the company; the chances are that he/she will have the ability to make it happen.

64

Become an intrapreneur – view your job as a consulting assignment, not a permanent gig

Think broader than your immediate job

An intrapreneur is defined as "a person who, while remaining within a larger organization, uses entrepreneurial skills to develop a new product or line of business as a subsidiary of the organization".[46]

There are a few things you can do to be regarded as an intrapreneur:

- Take initiative – do not always to be told what needs to be done.
- Possess a helicopter view – think broader than your immediate job.
- Demonstrate strategic thinking.
- Be able to solve problems well and quickly.
- Demonstrate a certain level of independence.
- Display ambition and a need for achievement.

Strategic Thinking[47]

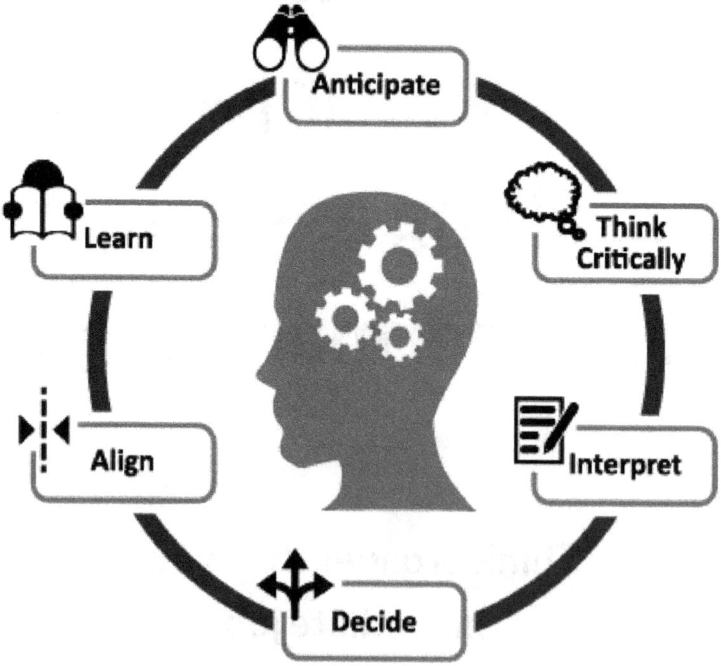

65

Do not be too cautious – take some risk

You need to take risks in order to progress

Be innovative. Take risks. Always be on the lookout for problems in the organisation and do your best to find solutions, even if they are not under your direct control. I can assure you that senior leadership will always want to meet the staff member who solved a problem. The person who said risk taking is for entrepreneurs and risk aversion is for employees lied to us. Even as an employee, you need to take risks in order to progress.

66

Ask for more work or more responsibilities

Do not be a well-kept secret

In any big organisation, there is always an ongoing and fascinating tension between the product manager and the marketing manager. I have sat in countless work streams with people who hold those positions and watching them clash is fascinating. Ordinarily a product manager is responsible for the whole product development life cycle, while the marketing manager is responsible for bringing the product to market and driving its adoption. Every time the product is not performing as anticipated, the two point fingers at each other. The product manager accuses the marketing manager of not marketing the product well, and the marketing manager says something like, “You can’t market a bad product. If the product is bad, no amount of marketing can help it”. What an amazing lesson for all of us in our careers. Yes, we must market ourselves aggressively (self-promotion is important), but let us also invest in ourselves to make sure we are GOOD products. Are you a good product? If you believe you are, then ask for more work. Do not be a well-kept secret.

Raising your hand to help out other departments or teams – or simply asking for more responsibilities – increases your value within the organisation. Asking for additional work shows an interest and desire to help your company to succeed. It also puts a spotlight on your value to the business.

Join a Professional Association relevant to you and when you get there, volunteer to do something

Associations look great on your CV

Associations look great on your CV and are helpful networks to tap into when searching for a job. Do not wait until you need the support; get involved right away and start building those relationships. My involvement at the South African Board for People Practices and at the Professional Speakers Association of Southern Africa has really contributed to my career growth. When I tell some people, they always say their employer refuses to pay for their membership fee. If I were you, I would just pay for myself – it is worth it.

Although each organisation has its unique advantages, most professional associations offer some or all of the following basic benefits:

68

Find a mentor inside your organisation and another one outside

Make sure your request for a mentor stands out

When it comes to selecting a mentor, the greatest likelihood is that the person you are considering gets many requests for mentorship, which is why you have to make sure your request stands out. Here are a few suggestions:

- Be an excellent performer in your current role. Every senior person wants to mentor a performer. If you cannot even do your job, maybe you should focus on that.

- Be persistent but not irritating – there is a very thin line here. Follow the correct channels and be polite, but do not give up when they decline the first time. Remember that the person does not owe you anything.

- Show them something you are currently busy with and ask for input or proofreading. This is much better than the 'coffee request' invitation. It shows that you are not just a talker, but also a doer.

- Make your proposal clear and be upfront about what is involved or required.

- When you eventually meet, shut up and listen. Many people use this opportunity to try to sell themselves and they waste the mentor's time. Humble yourself and learn.

69

You must perform but you must also be seen to be performing

Ensure that your performance represents you well

What is the use of doing something great for your organisation if no one will know about it? You must learn the art of self-promotion. I say 'art' because that is exactly what it is; you have to do it in a subtle manner while still accomplishing the goal. The trick is to be subtle yet effective, microscopic yet proactive.

You also have to select your crowd strategically by making sure the people who matter know what you have done. In corporate South Africa, talent meetings/forums are held regularly; make it your mission to ensure your name always appears there.

This is how not to do it: do not try to go over your boss' head by sending her boss emails; that is career suicide, so please find other creative ways to promote yourself. Many companies have sites where you can log innovative ideas, so use them. Attend every session where the CEO is updating staff on financial results etc. and ask relevant questions.

The point is to be visible everywhere while making sure you are performing. You do not want to be in the spotlight when your work and performance rating do not deserve to be. Your work must shine bright, so if you are to be seen and known, sloppy work and average performance cannot be associated with you. To stand out as your own personal brand requires that you simultaneously produce work that is worthy of the spotlight. Align the two by ensuring your performance represents you well.

70

Invest in your own development

You need to sacrifice to develop

When I was 25, I registered for an MBA, but because I was too junior to qualify for a bursary, I paid for it myself. Well, at least for the first two years. After doing well in those initial years, my employer decided to pay for the last year. When I told some people they commented that it was so expensive and wondered how I was able to afford it. These were the same people who wore really expensive shoes and paid R2,000 a month on clothes from a net salary of R4,800.

I was paying R2,000 for my education and my MBA has definitely added a zero or two to my annual earnings. Invest in your development, my friend – it always pays off so rather sacrifice the brands and top notch/'top shayela' lifestyle and resources.

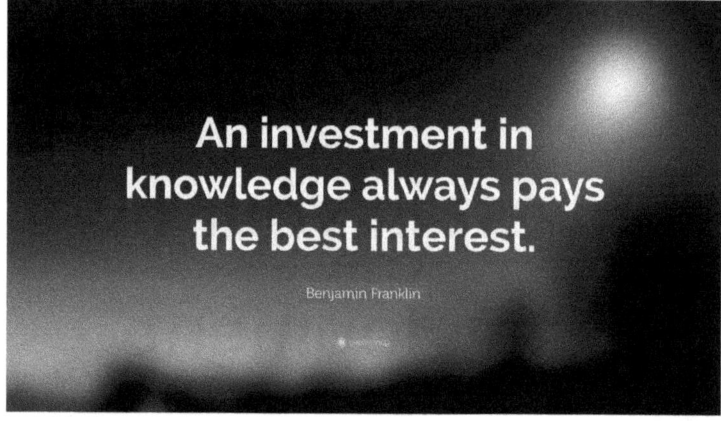

Speak for free at industry conferences if you have something to say

Raise your profile and position yourself as adding value

I am always amazed at a number of relatively senior people who do not do this. I mean, seriously, nothing says 'he's an expert' like speaking at industry conferences. Of course, you have to be relatively senior to do this, but if you are allowed to do it in your organisation, start now. It will raise your profile and position you as a value-adding employee.

72

Write articles and send them to the media all the time

Offer value and suddenly you are the 'go-to' person

Ask permission from your employers to write a regular article in 'your personal capacity' for newspapers and other professional and reputable sources of information. You can use this platform to discuss industry trends and give tips about relevant factors within your industry. What is interesting about this is that it allows you to shoot two birds with one stone by building your profile both in your company and in your industry at large.

Offer value and suddenly you are the 'go-to' person on that topic. Your internal bosses will struggle to ignore you if everyone outside is looking for you. The media will often want to know what you have published before they consider you, so the best way to start is by blogging. You can start your own blog for free and post interesting content. That will surely put you in a good place for consideration.

73

Update your LinkedIn profile

A LinkedIn profile is compulsory in this day and age

I am amazed at the number of people who do not have LinkedIn profiles. Those of us who are reasonably active on LinkedIn cannot even comprehend this. How can you say that you want to advance your career yet you do not even exist on this amazing platform? And then there is the second category of people who are registered there but all you see is their name and the company they worked for 10 years ago. Really? My friend, this is really easy to implement – do it immediately. An updated LinkedIn profile is compulsory in this day and age. In many recruiters' eyes, if you do not exist online, you simply do not exist!

Start dressing and behaving like a person at the next level

Show that you are ready for the next job

If your next level is an Executive Committee (EXCO) role, you must start observing how EXCO members in your organisation dress and behave. If they never take lunch breaks and only eat at their desks, do the same. If they wear a tie every day, start wearing one. If they carry a copy of the *Business Day* newspaper to work every day, subscribe and do the same. Even if you do not understand anything on the pages, read it – it will all start making sense eventually. Most significantly, however, you will be communicating a very clear message – I want that job and I am ready for it.

75

Work yourself out of a position to get a promotion

Be a leader by training others

Career progression can be a bit confusing; sometimes being the reliable specialist in your organisation can hamper your advancement. One way to outgrow your current position is by ridiculously excelling in it, i.e. doing it so well and without struggle. This proves a level of mastery and shows you are ready for greater challenges and responsibilities. However, a twist is that if you are the only one in your division who is a specialist in a particular system, why would management risk promoting you and losing that skill?

In this case, you must train other people. As the saying goes, 'If you're the only one who can do it, then you are not a good leader'. The point of leadership is empowering and enabling others to do it just as well, so be a leader by training others. Then, once there is someone else with the same ability or potential as you, show your seniors that there is more to you than they think. In this way, you show them that you can do far more than your current position and your promotion will not be considered a loss to your department.

76

Exit and return senior strategy

To be taken seriously, you have to leave and then return in a senior role

Sometimes in an organisation where you started as an Administrator, for example, people will always see you as an Administrator, no matter what you do. In this case, no matter how much you actually love the organisation, you must leave and get a senior role elsewhere. If you really love the organisation, you can always return years later as someone senior and you will be taken more seriously.

The downgrade to upgrade strategy

Work towards a better future

Let me create a scenario. Let us say that you completed a degree in mechanical engineering about five years ago, but because you were struggling to get a job or an internship in that field, you ended up taking a job as a Call Centre Agent at a bank. After three years of being an Agent, you were promoted to being a Team Leader and you now earn R10,000 per month.

Suddenly you are offered a mechanical engineering internship at a very big company for R6,500 per month. You have bills but you love mechanical engineering, and you know in the long run that you will earn more if you take the internship. What do you do? I suggest you use what I call the "downgrade to upgrade strategy". Take the internship, downgrade your lifestyle (sell your car, move into a backroom somewhere) and just start all over again. I know it is not as easy as it sounds, but trust me, you will be glad you did down the line.

78

Go horizontal to go vertical

It will be worth it one day

In some small organisations with a flat structure, getting a promotion can be very hard. This does not mean you cannot progress, it just means you must be willing to take certain jobs that are on the same level if they will enhance your experience. Sometimes you just have to go horizontal in order to go vertical – like a downgrade for an upgrade, it always pays off in the end. If you are currently working in a support function and have ambitions of becoming CEO/MD, consider moving sideways and even taking a small demotion into an operational role with Profit & Loss responsibility. It will be worth it one day.

79

Invest in a presentation/ communication skills programme

Develop and improve yourself

Why anybody still calls communication/presentation skills a 'soft skill' is a phenomenon I will never understand. Often the reason many people do not advance in their career is because they are really poor communicators. You might know your job in and out, but if you cannot communicate, your advancement will be limited.

Do not let this so-called 'soft skill' hinder your progress; read and write about anything that interests you and take a communications class – both theoretical and practical if possible. Read up on and attend effective communications forums that will give you an opportunity to present and receive feedback so that you can develop and improve yourself.

80

Know the degrees, universities and learning programmes that are valued in your company

You will improve your chances of advancement

I have worked as a Head of Learning/Training & Development in a few organisations and I can tell you this unequivocally... every organisation has degrees, universities and learning programmes that are held in high esteem. If you attend a certain programme or do a particular degree in that institution, you improve your chances of advancement in your organisation.

It is your job to know what these are for your organisation and it is not that hard to find that information. Senior Managers, Human Resources and Heads of Learning and Development know them – the time to have that discussion with them is here and now.

81

Speak up

Do not only speak when you have to give feedback

If you are going to attend meetings and keep quict for the entire session then the message is clear: you lack knowledge and there is nothing you can say that everyone else does not know. In order to be an active participant, you must first be knowledgeable about the subject matter and you have to speak up. Nobody really knows what you know, so it is important to share your knowledge.

Most organisations have project teams that meet regularly until their particular project is implemented. In these project meetings, you find representatives from all departments who are needed for the launch of the project. What an opportunity this is for people to know you and to know what you know. Do not only speak when you have to give feedback about your department; give other suggestions that could add value. A huge disclaimer though: you have to know what you are talking about otherwise you will achieve the opposite of what you intended.

82

Know more about the company, not just your division

There are always more opportunities than you think

When I worked for a big bank, I was always surprised by how little people knew about the company they worked for. Some people did not even know which cluster their business belonged to, yet claimed they wanted to progress in the company. What a shock! When you do not know a lot about your company, you tend to think that the only way for you to progress is for your manager to leave, die or something of that sort.

Let me take this moment to inform you that you do not have to wait for such a time, because there are always more opportunities than you think in your organisation. To have information access, however, you have to know the company you work for in and out. You have to study the annual reports, financial statements, newsletters etc. How else are you supposed to add value?

83

Understand your organisation's politics

To get ahead, you need to know which buttons to press

I was attending a seminar one day and the speaker said, "Make it your mission to understand who plays golf with who, who goes to church with who and who went to high school with who in your organisation." When I heard that I thought to myself, 'Surely this is an exaggeration; we are just there to work and nothing else'. I have since learnt that it is important not to be ignorant of workplace dynamics. I would not necessarily go to the lengths that other people go to, but it is important.

You see, understanding these relationships and dynamics will help you in your progression as it will inform you how to relate to different people and indicate who the most persuasive and influential people are. Surely you need to know that if you want to get ahead? Let us face it; sometimes, in order to get ahead, you need to know which buttons to press and how to press them, but how will you know if you are not aware?

84

Earn a certification and make a big deal when you do

Certifications tell people that you are on top of your game

If your industry has some kind of certification, get it and make it known after attaining it. There are a few examples I can think of, including the Chartered Accountant, the Chartered Marketer, the Master Human Resource Practitioner and the Certified Speaking Professional. These tell people that you are on top of your game, so if there are any available in your industry, be sure to acquire it and make it known once you do.

85

If you are dissatisfied with your job, do something about it

It is in your hands

According to a 2012 *Harvard Business Review* article, successful rising stars in management are also dissatisfied with their career growth. "Young high achievers – 30 years old on average, with strong academic records, degrees from elite institutions and international internship experience are antsy. Three-quarters sent out résumés, contacted search firms, and interviewed for jobs at least once a year during their first employment stint. Nearly 95% regularly engaged in related activities such as updating résumés and seeking information on prospective employers. They left their companies, on average, after 28 months."[48]

If you are dissatisfied, do something – it is in your hands.

86

Use social media productively

Social media can be a very powerful tool; use it wisely

A few months ago, I read a book entitled, *To Quote Myself: A Memoir*, which was written by Khaya Dlanga, who is the Chief Marketing Officer of South Africa's new data-only mobile network, rain. I find it fascinating that Khaya used social media to create a profile, be hired at some leading advertising agencies, and eventually become a leader in the marketing and advertising industry.

Khaya could not finish his diploma in Advertising due to financial constraints, but instead of wallowing in self-pity, he put his ideas out on the Internet – firstly on YouTube and then on Twitter, and look where he is now.

Here is a summary of his profile:

He has been awarded more than 15 advertising awards including Loeries, a Gold Cannes Lion, a Black Eagle and honorary membership in the University of the Witwatersrand Chapter's Golden Key Award. His YouTube videos have been viewed more than 6.5 million times and he has more than 12,000 subscribers to his channel, putting him in the top 5% of the most viewed and subscribed users in the world.

More than 460,000 people follow Khaya on Twitter (@khayadlanga) and he was named 'Africa's top blogger' by the Highway Africa Conference. He was named in Jeremy Maggs' book, *Annual 2008 on Advertising, Media and Marketing*, as one of the '100 most influential people in media', and was the *Financial Mails'* 2009 Ad Focus New Broom of the Year.[49]

If you still think social media is just 'social', then you are sadly mistaken. Social media can be a very powerful tool to use to springboard your career – use it wisely.

87

Get those recognition awards

Recognition makes you look good

Whether it is the South African Music Awards, the South African Women in Science Awards or any awards in your industry or organisation; if you are eligible, enter them. Recognition makes you look good on paper and puts you in the spotlight. The last time I checked, looking good on paper and being in the spotlight for the right reasons puts one in a very good position for career progression, so why not?

88

Never ever depend on your salary alone

Many people have left jobs they really loved due to financial pressure

I think that it is totally impractical to expect one employer to meet all your financial needs these days; it just does not work well anymore, so you have to find ways to supplement your income. Many people have left jobs they really loved due to financial pressure.

One day, I was attending a seminar in Soweto and the speaker, Dr Bernard Nwaka, said the following words, which provoked me:

> *"If your salary is the only source of income you have; you are bewitched. The person who pays your salary determines where you can stay, which schools your child can attend etc. That is total manipulation and control. It is witchcraft to live only by salary; we need multiple streams of income."*
>
> (Dr Bernard Nwaka)[50]

Globally, the 'gig economy', where people work for many employers simultaneously, is taking off. Personally I believe this is the future. In South Africa, the gig economy is still relatively uncommon compared to countries such as the United States, but it will come. In the meantime though, sell Tupperware, Avon, shoes and bags; do music part-time; open a retail shop and ask your son to work there – just do something.

You must, however, remember to chat to your manager and the Risk and Compliance Department to determine what is allowed in your organisation before you do it.

89

Know your value

Don't believe everything you think

When I started speaking, I was always asked to speak for free. It was important then, but I learnt very quickly that people would not hesitate to exploit me if I did not know my value. People will say to you, "Come and sing for free because so and so will be there and he might book".

In corporates, most prospective employees accept the first job offer they get because they are desperate. In most cases, the prospective employer would have been willing to revise the offer if they had just been asked. Know the value that you deliver.

They will try to use the "He's so humble" line to try and exploit your gift. It is a trap – do not fall for it. Those who are used to dealing with arrogant drama queens and kings struggle to understand those with a bit of humility. They mistake it for naïvety or stupidity.

Know Your Worth | Know Your Value[51]

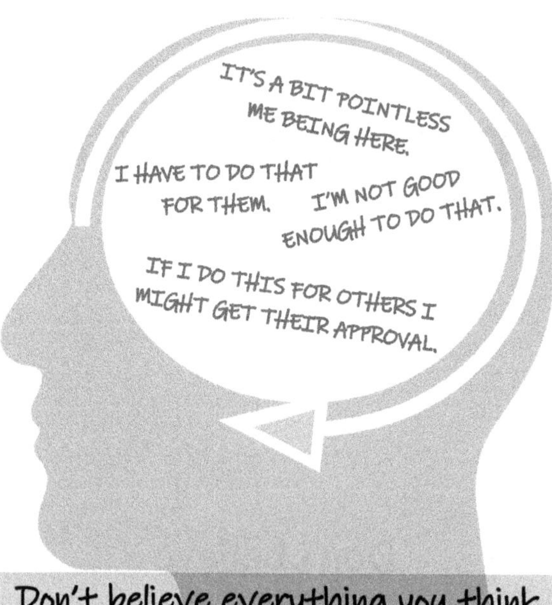

90

Do not let a performance rating stand in the way of your development

Focus on development outside of the normal performance cycle

My standpoint on performance ratings is simple. I strongly believe and advocate for separate sessions for a performance rating conversation and a development conversation. This is because in South Africa, and many other parts of the world, your performance score is linked to your increase, bonus and even career advancement opportunities. Because of this, a performance score becomes a huge determining factor and thus people fight very hard to get a good score.

In pursuit of a good score and the rewards thereof, honest developmental feedback is hindered, as you may not be receptive to it. For this reason, I believe it is best to schedule a one-on-one meeting with your manager where you focus on development outside of the normal performance cycle. In this way, you will be more open to feedback.

Performance Cycle[52]

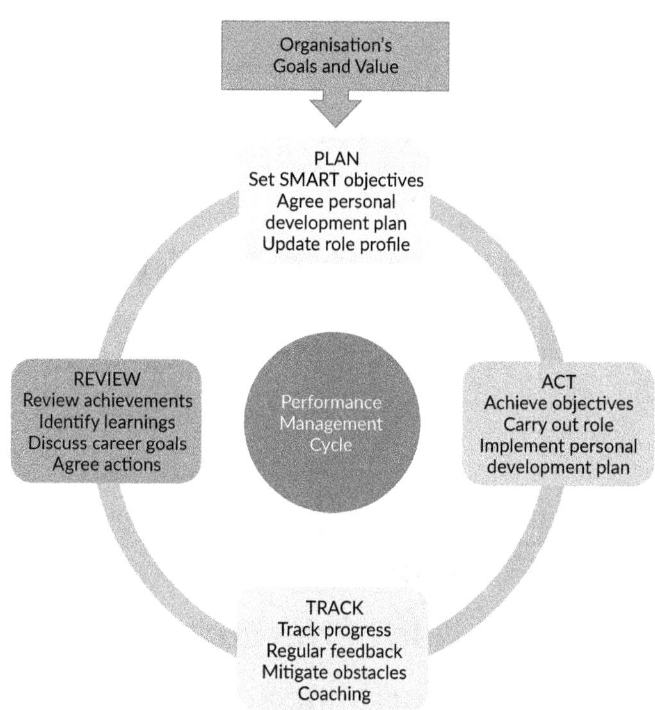

91

Do not work for one organisation forever

Do not disadvantage yourself by staying too long

Working for one organisation for a few years is great, but once you stay too long, recruiters and potential employers wonder if you are still agile enough to adjust to a new environment. Do not disadvantage yourself by working for one employer for too long.

In this day and age, you need to move with the times in order to keep up, so do not stay in one organisation as though you are a lizard trapped on a slippery surface. If you stay too long, it will be the only place you know and you will eventually be forced to leave, which in this case is likely to mean death, retrenchment or retirement.

92

Quantify your contribution to your organisation

Performance is the outcome of your behaviour

Many people, if asked, would not be able to explain clearly what their contribution to their organisation is. To address this, Human Performance Technologists emphasise the importance of quantification and documentation. Ever gone to that annual performance review discussion and relied on the fact that your manager knows what you have done? Well, that is not enough. You should be able to communicate, in output form, why you deserve a particular rating. Document and quantify.

As early as 1977, Fred Nickols observed that, "Behaviour is individual activity, whereas the outcomes of behaviour are the ways in which the behaving individual's environment is somehow different as a result of his or her behaviour". This is the sort of outcome your employer is interested in.[53]

In order to put this into practice, you need to adopt this mentality: performance is the outcome of your behaviour, it is not your behaviour itself. Therefore, focus on the outcome. Nobody cares what you have been doing, they care that what you have done has impacted the organisation. Avoid general statements and focus on specifics, i.e. numbers/quantifiable results. For example, you can explain that as a security guard you have reduced shrinkage by 22% year on year, which translates to a R4 million saving for the organisation.

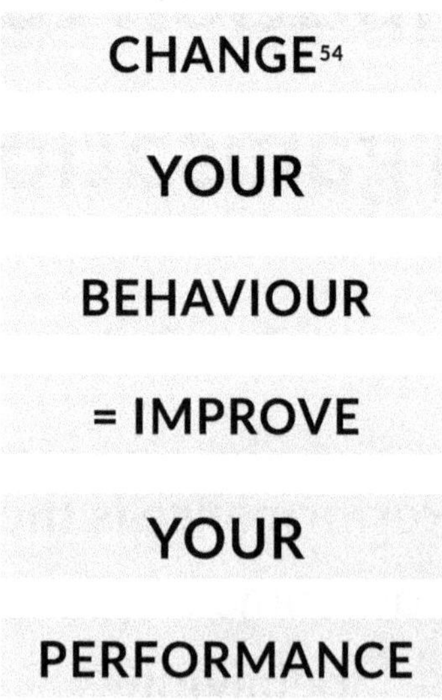

93

Eliminate the variables that may affect your job performance

Take care of the external variables to be an exceptional performer

In as much as I am an advocate of accountability and 'not blaming the system', the fact is that sometimes external variables may affect your performance, so you have to make sure all these are taken care of in order to perform. The HP Technologists suggest a few questions you can use to eliminate these variables:

a) Performance Specifications	• Do performance standards exist? • Do you know the desired output and performance standard? • Do you consider the standard attainable?
b) Task Interference	• Can your tasks be done without interference from other tasks? • Are the job procedures and workflow logical? • Are adequate resources available for you to perform (time, tools, staff, information)?
c) Consequences	• Are consequences aligned to support desired performance?
d) Feedback	• Do you receive feedback regarding your performance? • Is the feedback you receive: o relevant; o accurate; o timely; o specific; o constructive; and o easy to understand?
e) Knowledge/Skill	• Do you have the necessary skills to perform your role? • Do you know why the desired performance is important?
f) Individual Capacity	• Are you physically, mentally and emotionally able to perform?[55]

If any of these variables are not taken care of, it will be difficult for you to be the exceptional performer you can be, which will hinder your progress.

94

Get into the habit of analysing the biggest problems in your organisation and attempt to solve them

Acknowledge, diagnose, action and improve

There are many tools that you could use to diagnose problems in your organisation, however I suggest this process from Richard A. Swanson[56]:

a) Articulate your initial purpose – what is the issue?

b) Assess your performance variables.

c) Specify your performance measures.

d) Determine your performance needs.

e) Construct an improvement proposal.

Creative Problem Solving[57]

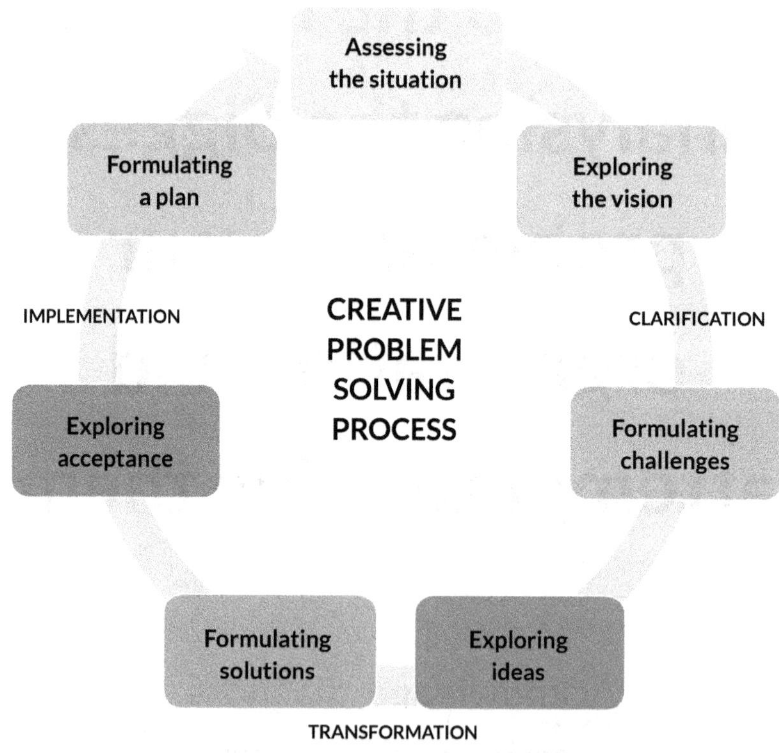

95

Acquire power/learn to influence

Intentionally acquire and build some power

Have you noticed how in every organisation, certain people wield power and therefore get things done, for example they have the ability to get their project on top of the IT implementation priority list? You can complain about this, or you could intentionally acquire and build some power. There are different types of power bases you can tap into, but most of the current theories about power use an analysis created by French and Raven over 40 years ago when they identified five principle sources or bases of power:[58]

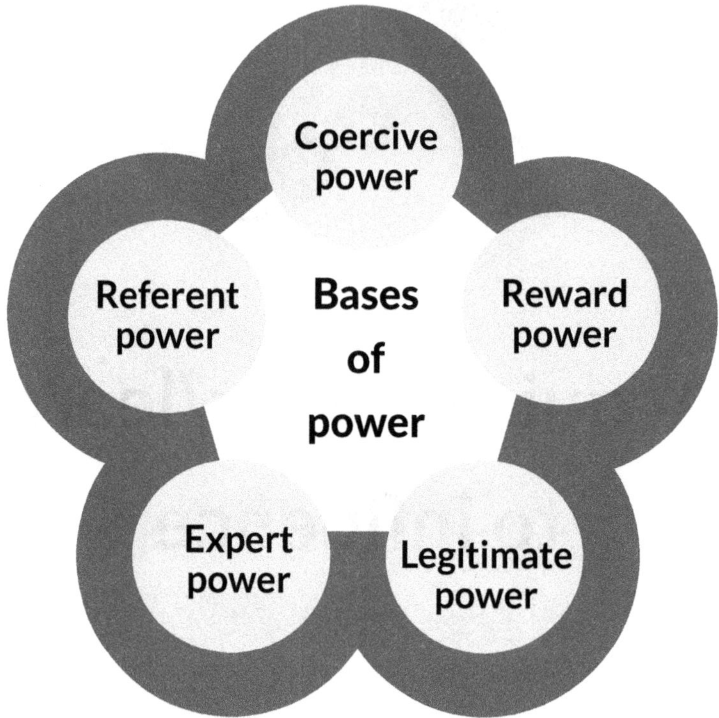

1. **Coercive power**

   The first is the crudest form of power, which uses threats and punishments to achieve its ends. These could include sanctions against suppliers, dismissals for non-co-operating staff, demonstrations etc. In my view, this source of power should be used as a last resort.

2. **Reward power**

   This refers to the use of rewards to influence people's compliance. To be effective, the rewards must be desired by the target group, e.g. financial inducements. In my experience, monetary rewards work but they have their limits.

3. **Legitimate power**

   Generally known as authority, this implies the power to act as well as power over resources.

4. **Expert power**

   This power comes from possessing specialist knowledge and skills, and is dependent on the recognition of expertise by those concerned. Credibility is vital otherwise no one will take any notice.

> *"Competence is a key to credibility, and credibility is the key to influencing others."*
>
> (John C. Maxwell)

5. **Referent power**

   Generally known as personal power or charisma, referent power comes from the high regard in which one is held by others. Should this falter or wane, this form of power vanishes, although it is often employed in conjunction with other sources.

Focus – there is something called too much diversification

Focus your energy on a few factors

Someone recently said to me, “I speak on culture, innovation, motivation, relationships, finances, future trends, HR and safety”. I wanted to say, “Oh, I see, you are a chancer”, but I did not. The fact about our human nature is that we need focus because we just cannot do everything. As mentioned earlier, to attain mastery on a single element requires a huge amount of time, so where does one get the time to master so many things? It is a mystery!

Trust me when I say that it is better to focus your energy on a few factors so you give yourself time to master them. In that way, you will not only achieve mastery and thereby find it easier to complete most tasks, but you will also have time for other significant things in your life such as family and ‘alone’ time.

Know who you are and do you

Do not emulate; differentiate

I am an avid follower of the South African entertainment industry. Not so much in the gossip and the frivolity that often accompanies show business, but as someone who studies and teaches career development, I love studying their career moves. Some of our celebrities are amazing strategists. Please allow me to give you an example. When a company decides to enter a new market, it is essential to use what we call a 'market penetration strategy' (business school language but please stay with me, I will explain). Think about some of the newcomers who managed to successfully penetrate the South African music industry in the last year or two. Think Mlindo the Vocalist, Sun El Musician and maybe Dladla Mshunqisi. Why were they able to penetrate such a crowded industry? I argue that they used a 'differentiation strategy' by utilising their unique sounds. I know people mock Dladla for the 'noise', but it is amazing how unique and distinct that 'noise' is. Differentiation distinguishes your brand from all the others. How did Nomzamo Mbatha penetrate the industry when people like Bonang Matheba, Minnie Dlamini etc. were dominant? Differentiation. She still has that "girl next door" vibe, even though she is monied and glamorous – incredible! Do you want to progress in your career? Then do not emulate; differentiate. The first step in being able to differentiate yourself is to have a high degree of self-awareness, which is what we are dealing with in this chapter.

Self-awareness is arguably the most fundamental issue in psychology, from both a developmental and an evolutionary perspective.[59]

Any career development is preceded by a deep search of who you are and the skills you actually have.

What is self-awareness?

The psychological study of self-awareness can be traced back to 1972, when psychologists Shelley Duval and Robert Wicklund developed the theory of self-awareness. From the ancient Greek aphorism, "know thyself", to western psychology, the topic of self-awareness has been studied by philosophers and psychologists alike for the last century. Simply put, self-awareness is an awareness of the self, with the self being what makes one's identity unique. These unique components include thoughts, experiences and abilities.[60] Daniel Goleman, in his popular book, *Emotional Intelligence*, proposed that self-awareness is "knowing one's internal states, preferences, resources, and intuitions".[61]

There are a number of great career development assessment tools and models, but all are essentially about answering the following questions:

- What am I passionate about?
- What is the deepest aspiration of my heart?
- What gifts and talents flow naturally to me? What is something I do well?
- What do other people see in me? What are they praising me for?
- What thoughts, visions and dreams are impossible to put out of my mind?
- What career would I feel peace in my heart pursuing?
- What could I give my all to for the rest of my life, even if I did not get paid?

These are some of the questions that really helped me to discover my gift of speaking and training, as well as my passion to help people develop in their careers.

98

Focus on your strengths, not your weaknesses

Find out what you do well and keep on doing it

Imagine your father giving you this advice: "Find out what you do well and keep on doing it." That is what John Maxwell's father used to say to him. Wow! Whenever you see people who are successful in their work, they are operating with their strengths, not their weaknesses.

One of the most important lessons I ever learnt when it comes to self-awareness, which I have applied in my career relentlessly, is to focus on my strengths not my weaknesses. It was in the mid-2000s when I first learnt about this concept of focusing on strengths, so I immediately decided to send the 20 people closest to me a simple text. It went something like this: 'I'm not searching for compliments, I'm doing an exercise on discovering my strengths: please let me know what you believe are my top three skills (something I do well).' The results were absolutely amazing. Every one of those people used words such as teaching, speaking, training and preaching. The only thing I am not doing on that list right now is preaching. The results when you choose to focus on your strengths are incredible. May I implore you to do the same exercise with the people closest to you? I would love to know the results you get.

There are many reasons why we should be focusing on our strengths; the following are just a few of them:[62]

- The strengths approach focuses on what is right, what is working, and what is strong.
- Every person in the world has strengths and deserves respect for those.
- Our areas of greatest potential are in the areas of our greatest strengths.
- We succeed by fixing our weaknesses only when we are also making the most of our strengths.
- Using our strengths is the smallest thing we can do to make the biggest difference.

What is a strength?

According to Buckingham and Clifton, a strength is a consistent, near perfect performance in an activity.[63] They added that a strength is a combination of three elements: talent, knowledge and skill. They defined each term as follows:

1. "**Talents** are your natural recurring patterns of thought, feeling, or behavior.
2. **Knowledge** consists of the facts and lessons learned.
3. **Skills** are the steps of an activity".[64]

How can I identify my strengths?

There are various tools you can use to identify your strengths. I would like to refer you to some websites that will help:

1. The first edition of *StrengthsFinder* by the father of Strengths Psychology, Donald O. Clifton, Tom Rath and colleagues at Gallup: https://www.gallupstrengthscenter.com.
2. Free VIA Assessment: https://www.viacharacter.org/.

99

Always pause and think – do not get into a rat race

Success is knowing your purpose in life

Every now and then, please pause and think about the meaning of life, the definition of success, and what is important. I often say that organisations are ruthless; if someone passes away on Thursday, they send flowers on Friday and start the recruitment process on Monday. Let us all look after ourselves, rest and take time out with our families.

There are many definitions of success but I really love this one by John C. Maxwell: "Success is knowing your purpose in life, growing to reach your maximum potential and sowing the seeds that benefit others. All of us have to define success for ourselves." In career development, we have a term for this; it is called having a protean career. The protean career is a name given to describe a career that is driven by the individual and not the organisation. The concept of the protean career dates to 1976, when in the book, *Careers in Organizations*, Douglas T. Hall noted an emerging type of career form that was less dependent upon the organisation in terms of defining success or achieving certain outcomes.

The most central characteristic of the protean career is that it is a reflection and manifestation of the individual career actor. An individual with a protean career – or one who is protean – is thought to put self-fulfilment and psychological success above concerns and norms that would have their source outside of the individual.[65] Psychological success is considered to be subjective success on the person's "own terms", in contrast to "objective" success that might be measured or defined externally (e.g., by salary or promotions). While a protean career might be identified externally as a definable career pattern, the literature and this entry are primarily concerned with how the career is enacted, managed, defined and evaluated from the individual's subjective perspective.[66]

If you take a job with a big salary but it makes you grumpy, moody, sick, a bad parent and just plain nasty, you are regressing. If you let go of a job that is detrimental to your health, you are not regressing, you are progressing. If you are now doing work that has a good career-life fit, you are progressing. If you are now doing work that makes you happier, you are progressing. If you are now doing work which is more meaningful to you, you are progressing.

100

Accept this fact: your career progression is in your hands

It is in YOUR hands!!!

There is a small village here in this beautiful continent of Africa. We are told a story that in this village, there was one village elder who knew everything that happened in the village and also seemed to have an answer for everything. Two young people from the village made it their mission to prove that this man did not know everything. They thought of a few ideas of how they could 'expose' him, until finally they settled on this one: they were going to capture two butterflies and then go to the elder holding them enclosed in their hands. Their plan was to ask the elder if the butterflies were dead or alive. If he said that the butterflies were dead, they would just open their hands and show him that they were alive, in that way proving that he was not as knowledgeable as people made him out to be. If he said they were alive, they would just squash and kill them, and they would have won. Eventually they went to him, asking if the butterflies were alive or dead. The elderly man paused for a few seconds and said to them: "Young people, whether the butterflies in there are dead or alive, is in your hands".

My dear friend, whether your career is dead or alive, it is in YOUR hands. Never delegate this responsibility to anybody else.

#StagnationMustFall

ENDNOTES

1 Maxwell, J.C. 2009. *Self-improvement 101: What every leader needs to know.* Nashville: Thomas Nelson.

2 Bussin, M. & Blair, M. 2019. *The New World of Work: An 'SOS' Call to Management*. Bryanston: KR Publishing.

3 Deloitte. 2017. *Global human capital trends.* Retrieved from: Bryanhttps://www2.deloitte.com/insights/us/en/focus/human-capital-trends/2017.html.

4 United States Bureau of Labor Statistics. 2018. *News release*. Retrieved from: https://www.bls.gov/news.release/pdf/tenure.pdf.

5 Statistics South Africa. 2016. *Labour Market Dynamics Report*. Retrieved from: http://www.statssa.gov.za/publications/Report-02-11-02/Report-02-11-022016.pdf.

6 Maxwell, J.C. 2009. *Self-improvement 101: What every leader needs to know.* Nashville: Thomas Nelson.

7 Gorbachev, M.S. 2011. Elbert Hubbard Quote in *Prophet of Change: from the Cold War to a Sustainable World*. Forest Row: Clairview Books, p.322.

8 Warren, R. 2016. *Why Your Way Isn't Working*. Retrieved from: https://www.crosswalk.com/devotionals/daily-hope-with-rick-warren/daily-hope-with-rick-warren-july-12-2016.html.

9 Maxwell, J.C. 2016. *3 Things Successful People Do: The Road Map that will Change Your Life.* Nashville, Tennessee: HarperCollins.

10 Blake, J. 2016. *Pivot: The Only Move that Matters is Your Next One.* New York: Portfolio/ Penguin Random House.

11 SlideShare.net. 2013. *Art of developing positive attitude.* Retrieved from: https://www.slideshare.net/varunchandok18/art-of-developing-positive-attitude.

12 Dostoevsky, F. 1917. Crime and Punishment. *The Harvard Classics Shelf of Fiction*. Retrieved from: https://www.bartleby.com/318/11.html.

13 Brothers, J. 2017. *The person interested in success has to learn to view failure as a healthy, inevitable part of the process of getting to the top*. Retrieved from: https://flavell.mit.edu/2017/02/22/person-interested-success-learn-view-failure-healthy-inevitable-part-process-getting-top/.

14 Tracy, B. 2002. *The Psychology of Achievement*. New York, NY: Simon & Schuster Audio.

15 Blake, J. 2016. *Pivot: The Only Move that Matters is Your Next One.* New York: Portfolio/ Penguin Random House.

16 Csikszentmihalyi, M. 1990. *Flow: the psychology of optimal experience.* New York: Harper & Row.

17 Mayberry, M. 2015. *20 Quotes to Help Motivate You to Hustle Like Never Before.* Retrieved from: https://www.entrepreneur.com/article/247859.

18 Maxwell, J.C. 2016. *3 Things Successful People Do: The Road Map that will Change Your Life.* Nashville, Tennessee: HarperCollins.

19 Duhigg, C. 2013. *The Power of Habit: Why we do what we do and how to change.* 19th ed. New York: Random House Books. Image retrieved from: https://medium.com/@laxmena/the-habit-loop-book-review-the-power-of-habit-303dc690825d

20 Barrie, J.M. n.d. *Dreams do come true, if only we wish hard enough. You can have anything in life if you will sacrifice everything else for it.* Retrieved from: https://www.goodreads.com/quotes/32357-dreams-do-come-true-if-only-we-wish-hard-enough.

21 Goodreads. n.d. *Quote by Anonymous.* Retrieved from: https://www.goodreads.com/quotes/7842132-if-you-don-t-sacrifice-for-what-you-want-what-you.

22 allBusiness.com. n.d. *Mastering "the Art of Getting Things Done Through People".* Retrieved from: https://www.allbusiness.com/mastering-the-art-of-getting-things-done-through-people-12023-1.html.

23 Goodreads. n.d. *Robert Greene Quote.* Retrieved from: https://www.goodreads.com/quotes/240846-law-4-always-say-less-than-necessary-when-you-are.

24 Tracy, B. 2001. *Get Paid More and Promote Faster: 21 Great Ways to Get Ahead in your Career.* San Francisco: Berrett-Koehler Publishers.

25 Quotation.io. n.d. *Quote by Steve Maraboli.* Retrieved from: https://quotation.io/page/quote/sense-entitlement-cancerous-thought-process.

26 Gladwell, M. 2011. *Outliers: The story of success.* New York: Back Bay Books.

27 Williams, M. 2017. *Personal and Professional Development.* Retrieved from: https://www.sales-mind.com/blog/personal-professional-development-essential-developing-self-confidence-success-life

28 Tracy, B. 2000. *The 100 Absolutely Unbreakable Laws of Business Success.* San Francisco, California: Berrett-Koehler Publishers, Inc.

29 Daska, L. 2014. *10 Toxic People You Should Avoid at All Costs.* Retrieved from: https://www.businessinsider.com/toxic-people-you-should-avoid-2014-10?IR=T

30 Covey, S. R. 2004. *The 7 habits of highly effective people: Restoring the character ethic.* New York: Free Press.

31 Collins, J. 2001. *Good to Great: why some companies make the leap ... and others don't.* New York, NY: HarperBusiness.

32 Mind Tools Content Team. n.d. *The Hedgehog Concept: Using the Power of Simplicity to Succeed.* Retrieved from: https://www.mindtools.com/pages/article/hedgehog-concept.htm

33 Collins, J. 2001. *Good to Great: why some companies make the leap ... and others don't.* New York, NY: HarperBusiness.

34 Ibid.

35 Ibid.

36 Venner-Pack, N. 2016. *Peer-to-Peer Career in the GIG Economy.* Retrieved from: https://www.rage.com.my/malaysia-gig-economy/.

37 Brainyquote.com. n.d. *Les Brown Quotes.* Retrieved from: https://www.brainyquote.com/quotes/les_brown_393475.

38 Quotefancy.com. n.d. *Austin Kleon Quote.* Retrieved from: https://quotefancy.com/quote/1720419/Austin-Kleon-Enjoy-your-obscurity-while-it-lasts

39 Goodreads.com. n.d. *Steve Goodier Quotes.* Retrieved from: https://www.goodreads.com/author/quotes/720214.Steve_Goodier.

40 Goodreads.com. n.d. *Dee Dee Atner Quotes.* Retrieved from: https://www.goodreads.com/quotes/1259657-blaming-others-is-an-act-of-refusing-to-take-responsibility.

41 Goodreads.com. n.d. *False Perception Quotes. Shannon. L. Alder.* Retrieved from: https://www.goodreads.com/quotes/tag/false-perception.

42 Benjamin P. Hardy Inc. 2017. *21 Behaviors that will make you brilliant at creativity.* Retrieved from: https://attackthefront.com/2017/once-you-desire-progress-more-than-convenience/

43 Martin, M., 2018. *Conduct a Personal SWOT Analysis to Improve Your Career.* Retrieved from: https://www.businessnewsdaily.com/5543-personal-swot-analysis.html

44 Sheppard, C. 2009. *The State of Youth in South Africa: Trends in Education Attainment.* Retrieved from: http://www.hsrc.ac.za/en/research-data/ktree-doc/1671

45 Glints. 2018. *Career planning in Singapore: A guide.* Retrieved from: https://glints.com/sg/hired/career-planning-singapore-guide/.

46 Intrapreneurship. (n.d.) *American Heritage® Dictionary of the English Language, Fifth Edition.* (2011). Retrieved from: https://www.thefreedictionary.com/Intrapreneurship.

47 Maris, D. 2015. *What's the difference between strategic thinking and strategic planning.* Retrieved from: https://www.lblstrategies.com/2015/08/01/whats-the-difference-between-strategic-thinking-and-strategic-planning/

48 Hamori, M., Cao, J. & Koyuncu, B. 2012. *Why Top Young Managers Are in a Nonstop Job Hunt.* Retrieved from: https://hbr.org/2012/07/why-top-young-managers-are-in-a-nonstop-job-hunt.

49 Bizcommunity.com. 2009. *2009 AdFocus winners.* Retrieved from: https://www.bizcommunity.com/Article/196/12/42538.html

50 Dr Bernard Nwaka. 2019. *Holy Spirit Seminar.*

51 Rural Grey Star. 2018. *Self-worth | Know Your Worth | Depression, anxiety, cfs/me warriors.* Retrieved from: https://ruralgreystar.com/self-worth/

52 Hearn, S. 2017. *Explaining the Stages of the Performance Management Cycle.* Retrieved from: https://www.clearreview.com/stages-of-performance-management-cycle/.

53 Nickols, F. 2012. *Concerning Performance and performance standards.* Retrieved from: https://www.nickols.us/opinion.htm.

54 Leibman, P. 2018. *Work Stronger: Habits for More Engergy, Less Stress, and Higher Performance at Work.* Förlag: Skyhorse

55 Rummler, GA. & Brache, AP. 2013. *Improving performance: How to manage the white space on the organization chart,* 3rd ed. San Francisco: Jossey-Bass.

56 Swanson, R. A. 1994. *Analysis for Improving Performance: Tools for Diagnosing Organizations and Documenting Workplace Expertise.* San Francisco: BerrettKoehler.

57 Korefacts. n.d. *Creative Problem Solving.* Retrieved from: http://www.korefacts.com/creative-problem-solving/.

58 Raven, B., & French, J. R. P., Jr. 1958. Legitimate power, coercive power, and observability in social influence. *Sociometry*, 21, 83—97.

59 Rochat, P. 2003. *Five levels of self-awareness as they unfold early in life.* Retrieved from: https://philpapers.org/rec/ROCFLO.

60 Zhuu, J. 2017. *What is Self-Awareness and why is it Important? 5 Ways to Increase It.* Retrieved from: https://positivepsychologyprogram.com/self-awareness-matters-how-you-can-be-more-self-aware/.

61 Goleman, D. 1995. *Emotional intelligence: why it can matter more than IQ.* New York: Bantam Books.

62 Linley, A. 2008. *Average to A+: realising strengths in yourself and others.* Coventry, UK: CAPP Press.

63 Buckingham, M. & Clifton, D.O. 2001. *Now, discover your strengths.* New York: Free Press.

64 Buckingham, M. & Clifton, D.O. 2001. *Now, discover your strengths.* New York: Free Press, p. 29.

65 Briscoe, J.P. & Hall, D.T. 2006. The Interplay of the Protean and Boundaryless Careers: Combinations and Implications (Forthcoming). *Journal of Vocational Behavior, 69*(1), 4-18.

66 Hall, D. T. 2002. *Careers in and out of Organizations.* Thousand Oaks, CA: Sage.

www.ingramcontent.com/pod-product-compliance
Lightning Source LLC
Chambersburg PA
CBHW071653200326
41519CB00012BA/2506